THE BLUE L

Valerie R. Peterson

MCCLURE PUBLISHING, INC.

Cover Design by Kathy McClure

To order additional copies, please contact:
McClure Publishing, Inc.
www.mcclurepublishing.com
800.659.4908

TABLE OF CONTENTS

The Blue Lotus

Foreword

Introduction

DEDICATIONS

This book is dedicated to my Dad Solomon Edward Peterson, my mentor Dr. Chandra Taylor Smith, my favorite cousin, Amron Thomas, and you the reader.

ACKNOWLEDGEMENTS

Special thanks to the following people who helped me survive to tell my story. You have blessed me more than you can imagine. Thank you for helping me survive the storm and get to the other side. I LOVE YOU and I HONOR You! I will never forget!

- Family: Stacey, Nicholas, Veronica, Kenedi, and Devin
- LTC (ret) Consuelo Kickbusch
- Greg Darnieder
- Pamela Norfleet
- Adrian Ivy
- Bernard McCune
- Carlton Griffin
- Cathy and Calvin Bryant
- Charles Garrison
- Colevon Kelley
- Denita and Denise Nixon
- Dr. Bernard Franklin
- Dr. Chernara Baker
- Dr. Heather Hampton
- Dr. Wendell Brown
- Drs. Bobbie and Arval Chappell
- Elder Charles and Rita Radcliffe
- Elder David and Evangelist Paulette Foster
- Evangelist Bobbie Barney
- Fenesha Hubbard
- First Sergeant Jack Harper
- G.B.
- Jean-Jacques Taylor
- Jolene Yoakum
- Kathryn Compton
- Latanya Searcy
- Lauren Bowen

- Lauren Ramers
- Lee Felts
- Leonard Freeman
- Lisa Terrazas
- Marilyn Gilbert Mitchell
- Marlon Ratliff
- Marqita Fitch
- Mary Beck
- Michele Welch
- Myles Ward
- Pastor Bill Ellis
- Pastor John Hannah
- Paulette Easton
- Rachel Henley
- Rebecca and Ron Edwards
- Rebekah Vereen
- Reggie Simmons
- Remi White
- Rev Jacqueline Hawkins
- Romona Johnson
- Rona Radcliffe
- Rosemary Ellis
- Ruthie Burch
- Ryan Adams
- Ryan Baggett
- Sergeant Grover Harper
- Shavon Fields
- Tommie and Tomika Harris

Your love, guidance, support, and patience with me in different phases of my life made this possible.

Thank you for being my angels.

"Your text has been completed. It's all here. There is nothing more humanity needs to hear to grow. There will be no new teachings, for they are unnecessary. What we, in spirit, are here to do is to point you to what has already been given."

"You live in a loving universe. All of the forces are here to give you assistance, to give you support."

"We admire you tremendously. Those of us who have been human know full well the courage it takes."

~EMMANUEL'S BOOK

THE BLUE LOTUS

The lotus is a gorgeous flower, but it endures an interesting process before you can see its beauty. The lotus blossoms on mud, which is dirty. The rainwater drops from the sky, meets what is left on the ground, takes those toxins, and turns it into a wet mess. In the mud, the lotus' root begins to form as oxygen and other nutrients support the lotus' growth.

For many of us, our lives mimic the lotus' life. There are tremendous opportunities for growth during our times of hardship. The question is whether we choose to wallow in hurt and pain or whether we choose to learn from life's lessons and move forward. I chose the latter.

Once the lotus starts to blossom and grow through all the dirt and mud, the end result is a beautiful flower. The lotus transforms and grows beyond the surface of the water many feet into the air. Not only does it grow and blossom, it's also able to use the excess mud used in its production to replicate itself to make more lotus flowers. How beautiful is that?

Despite the negative things we have gone through in life, we learn lessons and we have tremendous opportunities to grow. Not only do we grow, but we begin to know how to move forward in our life's journey.

The blue in the blue lotus represents the ocean and the nourishment of water which helps the lotus flower to grow. Blue is also calming. Yellow represents the sun. A source of light and a source of vitamins. The rays that come from the sun gently kisses my face.

FOREWORD

Lieutenant Colonel Consuelo Kickbusch (Retired)

Imagine a young girl from the Southside of Chicago finally about to graduate from High School, a feat considering her background, yet; there would be the memory of the End of Year Photo where she would have to put a Teddy Bear in front to hide one of her many struggles ... her daughter.

You may wonder did she quit, accept any job, or did she dare to go onto college once again to face the next struggle. College-ready she was not. Like many, Valerie was a young person who had been shackled with so much baggage such as abuse, poverty, low self-esteem, and being the victim. These name only some of the many trials she faced. Yet, she did have what so many with her circumstances lacked, FAITH and DETERMINATION.

Read this book to learn about the many other struggles, the wisdom gained, and how far her journey has taken her. She is still a "work in progress" or like I say to many mentees, "a diamond in the rough". Her VULNERABILITY is most honorable to read, and it makes her story so bittersweet like that of a Vidalia onion. If you have not had one, where have you been!

What she needed was more than just a mentor. Valerie needed a sponsor; someone who was willing to invest in her growth, future, and lay down a foundation of the HARSH TRUTHS she needed to embrace in order to leave behind the demons that haunted her most of her life. She was wearing the mask that many of us wear just to survive. She needed the mask to get to the next level and THRIVE!!

We have had our heavy doses of tough love and affectionately known "Conversations at the Kitchen Table" (what I like to call them), for I don't believe in enabling or confusing compassion with discipline and structure. Valerie reminded me of the many soldiers I have led and helped develop into the great leaders they were to become. I knew she had GREATNESS and BRILLIANCE in her, but it was clouded by a thick fog, composed of her mental struggles, pride, and trust issues.

We also had to get "over" the "color" conversations for we both are Women of Color; however, our heritage is different. It was in the richness of our deep conversations where we found the common grounds, the *aha* moments, and we both became Student and Teacher at the same time.

It is my HONOUR to be a part of Valerie's Journey and for however long I can walk with her, I shall remain grateful. Yes, the greatest compliment of any leader is to see the follower take the lead and make their history. As a servant leader, I know that day will come soon, and this book is the beginning of that step. So, I shall quietly pray and sing your praises.

Love you!

~CONSUELO

INTRODUCTION

During my life's journey, I have encountered things I wanted to know and things I did not want to know. Most importantly, I learned about myself. I am here to offer you a different way to process some things that trouble you. I will not replay my entire life to you, but I do want to inspire you and teach you about a path of my knowing which assisted me in releasing hurt. More than anything, I hope reading this book helps you consider the things you know, why you know them, and what you learned that you could use in your life moving forward. I'm pregnant, not in the physical sense, but I'm spiritually pregnant with a mission and a purpose.

This book represents a sliver of who I am. A look into pieces of my life. It is easier for me to talk about them now. When this happens, healing has occurred. I will never forget the events of my life, but they won't impact me the same. Life can be full of struggles. I learned the way you react within these struggles; determine how you will live the rest of your life. Do you want to be happy, or do you want to remain sad? This is a choice we must make. I now prefer happiness. This is a learned skill that requires you to let go. Learning how to push yourself out of the depth of despair is not an easy task. It takes will, it takes courage, and it takes time. Yes, we can wear a mask and look like everything is okay when it's really not. This is my story about rising out of my personal hell moments and being able to let go.

I believe. I trust. I let go! I remember this being the centering affirmation from several years ago when I participated in a daily meditation led by Oprah Winfrey and Deepak Chopra. The concentration of the meditation was accepting who we are just as we are, so we can align with our true purpose and ultimately our destiny. I say it all the time because it sounds good, and it makes me feel good. However, there were many moments in the past where I stopped and asked myself ... why say something, make it a part of my daily routine, and not believe it? It's not that I didn't want to but, when I looked at the truth of who I am, there was always an excuse, some doubt, some worry, some FEAR, or some reason why I could not ... and some reasons why I should not.

Now, I choose to view fear from a different perspective. For every awesome and wonderful thing, there were equally hurtful and painful moments. Moments that made me unable to clearly visualize my next steps. This led to me being afraid of moving forward. The good news is, there was a reason and a meaning behind them all. The better news is that, behind your greatest fear lies your greatest attribute that will birth all your hopes and dreams.

We live amid a vast, resourceful universe that knows and guides us. We have the responsibility to trust its guidance and let go of fear because all fear does is hold us back. In fact, it held me back from writing this book several times. Over the course of many years, there has been many starts and stops. Stops, because I didn't want to relive the pain of having to deal with the truth of who I thought I was, who I had become, and who I am.

Now, I realize there will never be a "best" time because time doesn't exist the way we were taught it does. So, I surrendered, I let go. In this moment and in this space, I know I am right where I am supposed to be. You're right where you're supposed to be which is learning how to recognize the healing process. Throughout the course of me writing this book and you reading this book, my intentions are for us to become empowered and accomplish more than we ever imagined. I want us to discover and to listen to our truth and know who we really are.

At the end of this book, I hope that all self-imposed limitations are released, and we become free to produce what is in our creative mind.

We are still on our journey called life and no matter what, all is well. It's hard to say all is well when you're in a situation that causes you to continually ask the question 'why'. Why is a good question but if you don't seek the answer, the 'why' will remain. I took time to reflect over the many journals that I have used throughout the years. I wondered about where I am right now versus how I was back then. I then asked myself a question. What did I learn and what haven't I learned yet. This is about the painful moments of my life that I learned to look at from a different perspective. This is about how I made it through those moments and how I am able to tell my story. I hope that you will find inspiration and become empowered to reflect on your personal moments and work towards healing.

Answer this: What do you hope to gain by reading this book?

_____

_____

_____

_____

_____

_____

_____

_____

_____

_____

_____

_____

_____

_____

_____

_____

<u>Journal Entry</u>

"Today I recognize it's not all about me. There are tons of
other people and things I can support. I'm aware it is time
for me to do some things I may be uncomfortable with. I
know there's continued healing and freedom in being
aware. I have faith and all is well. This is my healing
journey, a process I will continue forever."

~VALERIE

THE JOURNEY IS IN THE JOURNALING

2015 ends and 2016 begins. I left the first page of this journal blank as a reminder I get to start over again, I can be renewed and refreshed. I am leaving the past behind and looking forward to bold and big things God is ready to provide. I am looking forward to the love and the laughter to share with others. I am grateful for all the lessons learned and to apply the learning to get back on track. The last five months have been extremely difficult, but I know the next 12 months will be full of awesomeness and excitement. I am grateful.

~VALERIE

Journaling is a great communication tool for yourself. While it's often used to jot down your day-to-day thoughts and activities, it can also be a powerful tool for reflection. I have been journaling/writing letters since I was a child. I have kept all of my journals. I use them to go back and remember where I was at a particular point in time. It's how this book came to life.

In reviewing my journals, I noticed, I have done the same things over and over again expecting different results, which is also the definition of insanity. I have learned there are past pains I can genuinely say I have healed from, just like there are things I continue to heal from. One of the things we must understand is, the life we have is a life full of purpose. However, the direction in which purpose comes from is often unknown to some individuals. We can feed it or starve it. In my case, I have fed a lot of things, I fed it through marijuana, I fed it through vodka, and I fed it by sleeping and not caring for my health. I now take full responsibility for trying to avoid feeling what I needed to feel. It's easy to place the blame elsewhere. However, the driver of this lifeboat is me. Just like you are the driver of your lifeboat.

Journaling is essential to healing. It's your best friend. It has the notes you wrote about yourself to yourself over time. It's how this book came to be. The pain of living with the mask on is overwhelming, but where does the mask come from? For me, the mask came from pretending I had everything together. Pretending everything was great in my life when it was not. Pretending I knew what to do every time, and thinking I had control over every situation. It's easy to live a lie, it's harder to live the truth, to be open, to be honest, to be vulnerable. At some point you have to ask yourself, "Will

I live, or will I die?" For me, I choose to live and carry my baggage right in front of me. Living authentically, living free and whole, not caring what others think. There will always be ups and downs in life. The question is, how do you handle them?

I have a lot of journals. A journal for gratitude where I write what I'm thankful for every day even if it's *I'm thankful for breathing.* I have a dream journal to write out my dreams in the morning. I also have a general journal to jot down my thoughts and reflections of the day. When there are specific experiences I am having, I use a separate journal to write about those experiences. I keep all my journals and use them to see where I have grown and to discover areas where I need additional support. Journaling helps with your self-discovery, focus, as well as stress relief.

* * *

I use vision boards to create my reality. Things I desire are placed on the vision board. If you want a new job, find an artifact that represents it and place it on your board. You can use a poster board, paper, or even create one online. Over time, the visions I have placed on my vision board have come true. I learned this by reflecting on my vision board as well as my journals. I review my vision boards and journals frequently.

Realize it takes time and dedication to manifest your desires. You cannot create a vision board and expect everything will happen right away. Every year, I create a new vision board. The things that have not happened (*i.e.*, like me being able to pay off my student loans with one check) gets transferred to the next board.

We must remember that what we want is not going to fall in our laps. Not only do we have to speak into existence what we want and put it in front of our views, we have to put action behind them to see them happen. Thus, we have to put our goals into action by defining and completing the steps it takes to reach them.

Have you ever journaled? Why or why not?

_____
_____
_____
_____
_____
_____
_____
_____
_____

If you do journal, what have you learned about yourself?

_____
_____
_____
_____
_____
_____
_____
_____
_____

What is your purpose?

_____

_____

_____

_____

_____

_____

_____

_____

_____

_____

_____

_____

_____

_____

_____

_____

_____

_____

_____

_____

_____

_____

_____

_____

_____

_____

_____

_____

_____

_____

Message from Journal:

I am in a place of despair as I write in my journal, but quickly I receive direction.

> *Dear God,*
>
> *My life is in a chaotic state. My emotions are unstable, and I feel alone. I have no coping mechanisms that are healthy. I've been overspending, mixing drugs and alcohol, and wanting to stay to myself.*
>
> *Just about everything frustrates me. I'm aware of the areas of my life that are not in order.*
>
> *The first begins with my relationship with you. I know you're by my side, but I continue to fail and continue to seek your guidance. This is why I'm writing to you now. I need you. I need to feel your love.*
>
> *I need to be forgiven just as I need to forgive ... I surrender all to you. I also give to you the grief of my life as I can no longer carry the burden. I give to you the frustration and unknowing about my daughters and how I can pay for them to go to college. Please also take the heartache of worrying about my daughters and how they are feeling emotionally and what their futures look like.*
>
> *God, please control and remove the thoughts of not having enough or not being enough. Remove the stress of my student loan debt and remove the stress of the credit card debt.*

Remove the act of overspending and not saving, the overwhelming feeling of too many bills and not having and being enough.

God, refill my confidence and my glow ... and my ability to hear you and to listen to voices of reason for I know you can take the burden off of all of these things.

Heal my woundedness and make me whole so I can glow again. Let my confidence shine so much it blinds the eyes of people. Let it be so! That's it for now.

Now write your vision, make it specific and start planning what's needed to reach that vision. As hard as this may seem, you got this ... I'm right beside you.

KNOWLEDGE

No knowledge is knowledge unless it's lived and experienced
~OSHO

I believe the most valuable thing in life is information. It's all about what you know, how you know, and what action will you take to change your story?

"You feel me?"

"I got you"

"I KNOW you."

These are terms of 'understanding' that are exchanged between two people. From my experience, 'you feel me' can be explained as a feeling two or more people experience when they've had mutual situations happen to them. 'I got you' is a term in which a promise is suggested. For instance, someone can have your back

31

to protect you, or someone can offer to cover the bill in the restaurant. Basically, someone is expressing their willingness to be there for you and cares about your well-being in any situation.

To say 'I know you' is used too commonly. What you 'know' about me is from your perspective and is based on how much I allow you in. We also use 'know' to talk about habits in a negative manner to scold or correct. In those instances, we may say, 'you know that's not right' or 'you know better'. It is important to keep in mind, everyone sees the world from their own perspective based on their personal experiences.

My questions for you are:

Do you really know a person, or do you 'think' you know someone?

How authentic and transparent can you be with those you love so that you can help them see things from your perspective?

_____

_____

_____

_____

_____

_____

_____

_____

_____

_____

_____

Having a 'theory' about a situation versus experiencing it are two different things. Theory is a term often used scientifically. In order for a scientific theory to be proven, there must be tests that takes place. Either you test the theory and it's true, or you test it, and it's false. With experience, there is no test. The difference between testing a theory and experience is, experience allows you to gain a realistic application of knowledge. Belief gained from theories and tests don't have a solid basis.

Oprah Winfrey's book "What I **KNOW** for Sure" is among the most impactful books I've ever read. I've read and listened to it several times to reflect on the things I know and why I know them. **KNOW-LEDGE** is defined as, "facts, information, and skills acquired by a person through experience or education." The root word **'KNOW'** is the focus of this book. What do I know and how do I know it? When we **KNOW** something, we have left the realm of belief and have entered the realm of personal, intimate experience with 'some-thing'. Only at this point do we have facts and experience that speaks to 'why' we 'KNOW'. Instead of 'do you understand' the statement should be "help me understand." This is what creates the confidence in the knowledge we have obtained based on past experiences.

Knowing can apply to general things we encounter and experience in life. For example, I KNOW there is a God, a higher being is here to comfort and love us. I know this because I have felt the presence of God through prayer and meditation. I have an open line of communication which connects me directly to the source.

Knowing can also be specific. For example, I know I don't like to eat fish, especially catfish. I know this because I have tasted it, choked on some bones, and spit it out. However, I cannot say I like caviar. I have never tasted it, never had it before. This simply means the general statement such as 'I don't like fish', is not completely factual. I can believe I don't like caviar. I have an overall distaste for fish, however, the only way for me to know I don't like a specific type of fish is to taste it.

There's a remarkable story about Gandhi and a boy who ate sugar every day. The story goes something like this:

A woman was with her son and wanted to speak to Gandhi. So much so she waited in line for more than a day. The woman finally saw Gandhi and she said, "Mahatma please, tell my son he must stop eating sugar." She then begins to speak of the sickness her son was experiencing because of the sugar. She tried everything she could, to get her son to stop eating sugar. She told Gandhi he was a good boy but when it came to sugar, he would lie, cheat and steal. She asked Gandhi to make him stop. Gandhi looked at the boy for an exceptionally long time and then told the mother to come back in two weeks. Two weeks later the woman returned to Gandhi with her son and says, "Mahatma, we have returned, we came to you for help, but my son is still eating sugar." Gandhi remembered the mother and her son, he then asked for the son to come to him. Reluctantly, the boy went to Gandhi. Gandhi then looked the boy directly in his eyes and said firmly, "Don't eat sugar." The mother became upset and asked Gandhi why he could not tell him two weeks ago. Gandhi replied, "Two weeks ago, I was still eating sugar myself."

There is a difference between knowing something and believing something. Knowing is based on facts. Facts come from experience. You cannot talk the talk if you have not walked the walk in your own shoes. When you know something, you don't question it. You stand firm in knowing and move accordingly confidently. When you say you know something, you become accountable for the statements that follow. *For instance:*

- I know what it's like to being adopted and not know who my biological parents are.
- I know what it's like to be the youngest and the spoiled brat.

- I know what it's like to be born and raised in a Pentecostal Church.
- I know what it's like to be bullied.
- I know what it's like to be kicked out of a school.
- I know what it's like to be the ugly girl with the glasses.
- I know what it's like to be the nerd.
- I know what it's like to be raped.
- I know what it's like to have a sibling incarcerated for over 20 years.
- I know what it's like to be a teen Mother.
- I know what it's like to have an abortion.
- I know what it's like to be a single parent.
- I know what it's like to be betrayed.
- I know what it's like to be clinically depressed.
- I know what it's like to have anxiety.
- I know what it's like to see a psychiatrist.
- I know what it's like to go through withdrawal from Psychiatric meds.
- I know what it's like to be a first-generation college student after being told by some of the teachers and counselors in my High School to drop out.
- I know what it's like to work full time, go to school full time, and raise two daughters.
- I know what it's like to move from state to state, city to city in order to create a better life for my daughters.
- I know what it's like to be fired.
- I know what it's like to be codependent.
- I know what it's like to have borderline personality disorder.

- I know what it's like to be single, married, and divorced.
- I know what it's like to be in unhealthy relationships.
- I know what it's like to lose a parent.
- I know what it's like to lose a baby.
- I know what it's like to suffer from post-traumatic stress disorder.
- I know what it's like to receive therapy.
- I know what it's like to be diagnosed with Bipolar 2 disorder.
- I know what it's like to live paycheck to paycheck.
- I know what it's like to have multiple payday loans at the same time.
- I know what it's like to declare bankruptcy.
- I know what it's like to be in student loan and credit card debt at the same time.
- I know what it's like to rely on the assistance of the government to provide food, shelter, childcare, cash assistance, and healthcare.
- I know domestic violence.
- I know what it's like to have thoughts of suicide and actually attempt it.
- I know what it's like to not love myself.
- I know what it's like to have unhealthy coping mechanisms.
- I know I'm a work in progress.

* * *

The point is, I KNOW trauma. I learned and now KNOW how to free myself from the bondage trauma can create.

Knowledge is personal and everyone has a different level of knowing. This does not mean the knowledge we gained is right or wrong, but what it does do, is allow us to be mindful of how everyone comes to their conclusions from their own experiences.

Opposites attract for a reason, and it's not all bad. Opposites attract because there is learning that must take place. The purpose is to support one another because we need each other.

To support one another, we have to address these issues and know that it's okay to do that. We cannot be afraid of what other people think because it prevents us from speaking our truth. There are aspects of my life some can relate to, some not. My purpose is to help you reflect on those aspects of your life in which we have had similar experiences. Are you in it right now? Are you working on it? KNOW you are not alone. Me and millions of others have experienced trials and trauma or are currently going through them, so don't lose hope because we all had to learn.

The following are a list of things I learned about myself through my own trauma:

- The essence of who I am is beautiful, which is my ability to be soft and gentle.

- It is okay for me to connect with my inner child and to go on play dates and have fun.
- I am full of wisdom.
- I can breathe.
- Abundance flows easily and freely through me.
- I am free.
- I create my reality.
- Serving others serve me.
- I play. I create. I succeed.
- Joy is my highest purpose.
- I am a powerful creator.
- I have more than enough.
- We have to live in the present. We cannot go backwards. We have to live now.
- Suspend ego! Live out the center and work from there.
- I am imperfect and I am enough!
- What's shareable is bearable.
- I can always begin again.
- I am worthy of being loved.
- I am powerful.
- I forgive myself. Everything happens in divine order. There is space for me.
- My heart is my safe space. Yes and no will be much clearer on how to make decisions.
- I attract people that honor and respect the person that I am.
- I am strong.
- I don't need to rely on drugs or alcohol to suppress my feelings.
- I will no longer settle for less than what I'm worth.

- If somebody has to be happy, it's going to be me.
- I love and trust my imagination. I enjoy the creative process.
- I am a thought leader.
- I am classy.
- I am a connector.
- I advocate for the rights of all humans.
- The world is waiting for my vision.
- I learned how to cope mechanisms in more healthier ways.
- I am resilient.
- I am unapologetically me.
- How to heal from different types of hurt, pain, and trauma.
- I know how to better relate to others.
- The courage and strength to address the tough things I may encounter during the day.
- How-to live-in reality and the present moment.
- How to get out of a dark place.
- Self-Care comes first.
- I prefer spirituality over religion.
- I believe in the art of healing.
- I produce positive energy.
- I understand the importance of mentors and sponsorships as support mechanisms.
- How to speak out and loud to others.
- How to ask for help.

What you know is based on your experience. We need negative experiences or ones that we are not fond of to learn and grow. Without those experiences, we really don't know. Oprah's book, "What I Know for Sure" pushed me to think about how I would answer the question. As I thought about it repeatedly, I could not come up with anything concrete as I was still searching for answers. This is why I read and listened to the book numerous times. I needed to do deep introspection to find out. When I coupled it with my journals, I knew that I had a story to tell about what I know and why I know it.

People often say that they are an open book. I too, am an open book. I am publicly sharing my experiences, so I know I am not alone. I don't have anything to lose and holding in information is more stressful than helpful.

Create a list of your difficult experiences and a list next to it of all the positive things/lessons that you have learned from those experiences.

Difficult Experiences	Lessons Learned
Example: The loss of a romantic partner.	Example: What I need versus what I want.

Difficult Experiences	Lessons Learned

HUMBLE BEGINNINGS

*You don't choose your family. They are God's
gift to you, as you are to them.*
~**DESMOND TUTU**

I was born and raised on the far southside of Chicago.
I like to say I grew up in Roseland; however, my Mother
would argue it's West Pullman. Regardless, people
dubbed my area 'The Wild Hundreds (100's). It was
called The Wild 100's because of the gang territories,
violence, drug deals, shootings, car jackings, among
many other things that happened nearly every day. My
Mother stayed at home for the first part of my life which
allowed her to care for my sister, my brother, and me. My
Dad was a bus operator for the Chicago Transit Authority
(CTA), a job he loved and used to support our family.

I was the smarty pants of the family. My sister and my
brother were always getting into trouble at school. I
loved going to school. I loved reading. I loved teaching my

stuffed animals, and I loved watching Mr. Roger's Neighborhood and a little bit of Soul Train with my dad. I was a sickly child. I was frequently hospitalized for severe asthma and had difficulty with my vision. I have astigmatism and a lazy left eye.

I was picked on a lot as a child. Now that I'm older and can reflect, I probably would've picked on me too. I had a very juicy Jheri curl, huge glasses and essentially no style. I looked and felt different. I received special attention because I was special.

I would like to think I was vibrant, innocent, and free-spirited. Actually, I was quiet, shy, and conservative. I never wanted to do anything to draw attention to myself. I am all right with being plain in my appearance and did not and still till this day don't wear high heels. Comfortability reigns in my style book, even if that means wearing Crocs on my wedding day, which I did.

*   *   *

My Mother, Veronica, was born in Mobile Alabama to Ruth Logan and Robert Johnson. She came from a large family which consisted of three brothers and five sisters. My Mother suffered from a severe form of endometriosis and wound up having a total hysterectomy at 25 years of age. She longed for children. My Dad, Solomon, who was born in Chicago, Illinois became a foster child at the age of two. Before leaving for the military, he had been shuffled in and out of three different foster homes. My Father's Mother had a severe mental illness which prevented her from adequately caring for him. Having experienced the pain of being from a foster home, my

Dad didn't want any other child without a parent to go through the system without a permanent home. So, my parents decided adoption was the best option. They adopted a girl, Stacey, first and then they added a boy, Nicholas. Though Solomon and Veronica thought their family was complete, there was one more little girl waiting to be adopted.

Solomon and Veronica received a phone call from the adoption agency they were working with at Catholic Charities. A new baby needed a home, and the foster-care agent believed the baby resembled Solomon. We had the same espresso-colored skin tone, our eyes were almond-shaped and our noses were similar. The adoption agent believed I could physically pass for being Solomon and Veronica's biological baby. The agent begged them to come see the baby. On February 22, 1979, Solomon and Veronica Peterson welcomed their third adopted child – Valerie – into their home. Instantly, I had a new home, new parents, and new siblings. Growing up in a two-parent household was truly a blessing.

*   *   *

The first relationship we have is with our birth Mother. In the womb we eat what she eats, feels what she feels. We absorb energy through the umbilical cord which connects both mother and baby. For the first nine months of my existence, I incubated in a stranger's womb. On the day I was born, the first box on my birth certificate was left blank. I was taken into foster care and for two weeks, I was known as "Baby Davis." I have no clue of whose blood flows through my veins. I have no family history which also means I have no health history. I am adopted. My healing crisis began while I was a tiny seed in my biological Mother's womb.

"Who am I?" seems to be a simple question, yet it's difficult to answer. Physically, most of us know who we are and where we come from. We know the woman who gave birth to us and in most cases, we know our fathers. We have grandparents, aunts, uncles, cousins, nieces, and nephews. We know the chronic illnesses and diseases that runs in our family. Psychologically, we may have an idea of who we are as individuals. However, I believe most of us allow others to define us, while some of us acknowledge we are on a constant journey of discovery.

The narrative of my birth records is sealed, which means I have no access to information about my biological parents. However, in May of 2010, the State of Illinois passed House Bill 5428 which allowed any adopted person born after January 1, 1946, to obtain a non-certified copy of their original birth certificate. Because of the backlog of requests, I did not get my birth certificate until 2012. I found out my birth Mother's name and her age. My birth Father's name is not on the document. All I know about him is he was 22 years of age. I don't know and will probably never know why I was put up for adoption. In a sense, I say abandoned.... I don't know why I was abandoned. Abandoned is a strong word and may not even be the case. However, that is how this part of my life shows up in my mind frequently. My birth Mother could have been forced to put me up for adoption. I could be the result of a rape. The point is, I don't know. All of my life I have created stories in my mind to figure out my origin. What's in my blood? What's in my DNA? Do I look like my biological Mom or my Dad? Do I have any brothers or sisters who look like me?

Every single time my birthdate comes around, I wonder if my birth Mother thinks about me. What is my birth Father doing? Does he even know I exist? Or have I been forgotten? Hell, is my birth Mother still alive? Has she ever tried to find me? I don't know the answers to any of those questions. What I do know is I am curious and open to learning more about my genealogy, yet at the same time I feel it does not matter as God has fulfilled the void in my life. I don't have hate in my heart; I don't have any regrets. However, I do want to publicly let my birth Mother know *regardless of the circumstances, I forgive you and I am always open and ready to know you if you want to know me.*

People often tell me that I have a familiar face that I look like so and so. The question I ask myself *are they a biological sibling, cousin, uncle, aunt or relative?*

LETTERS FROM THE INSIDE

I love my brother dearly, but I did not see my brother often. I know some things about his journey including the fact he has been incarcerated for more than 20 years. Having an incarcerated sibling gave me a realistic view of how the criminal justice system really works. As a teenager, my brother became a gang member. Doing so, meant he began behaving in ways which did not reflect our upbringing. As a teenager, he was housed in the Juvenile Justice Center before being transferred to the Illinois Department of Corrections.

My parents tried hard to get my brother legal assistance. Ultimately, they mortgaged our house to pay for a bad lawyer. My parents could no longer afford a skilled defense attorney to handle my brother's litany of cases. As a result, we had to rely on public defenders who had little personal interest in Nicholas. My brother often accepted plea deals to avoid going to trial.

My brother has been housed in at least twelve different Illinois prisons, ranging from low-security to high-security facilities. Most were located three to nine hours away, which made visiting difficult. To drive that far only to see my brother for a couple of hours, was energy-sapping. The exhilaration of the morning drive to see my brother was often turned to frustration and exhaustion by the trip home. Sometimes, we could do it in a day; other times we could not. Occasionally, the facility would get locked down. When this happens, inmates are kept in their cells for 23 hours a day. Yes, they allowed visitation, but we would have to sit face-to-face with my brother as he sat handcuffed behind a thick slab of glass. We did not want to see him that way.

Arriving at the prison fascinated me – at least until I walked beyond the gates. The barbed wire fences. The tower guards. The inmates. All of it ... fascinating. It was, after all, a completely different world within our world. Upon arrival, two security doors had to be unlocked to let visitors in. Each heavy metal door clanged behind us as we passed through them on our way to the reception desk.

At the reception desk, we provided two forms of identification: a driver's license or some other government identification and birth certificate for kids under 18. No ID, no entry. Several times, we made the trip, but we could not see him because of 'something', and—the something—often varied.

In the waiting area, you could buy a card for a dollar which we used to buy snacks from the vending machine.

You could add a desired amount of money to the card. We would give it to my brother, who used it to enjoy his favorite snacks and meals. However, before we were allowed beyond the security area, several other procedures took place. Before being searched, we usually went to the restroom because once we were in the visitation room, we would need permission and an escort to get back out for any reason. To get back inside the visitation room, we had to go through a security check as before.

On the opposite side of the heavy prison doors was a locker room, where we placed all of our belongings. Then a female officer checked our bodies from head to toe for contraband. After the search, we went through a metal detector. From there we would be escorted outside and through several other doors before entering the visitation room filled with metal tables. Each table had four stools, one marked for the prisoner and three for visitors. If you had a baby or child, they had to sit on someone's lap. A guard sitting or standing at a podium would scrutinize every person. There was a backdrop for pictures and tons of board games, regular playing cards, UNO cards, and coloring books.

The expectation of seeing my brother was always exciting until I learned it would take at least an hour for my brother to come into the visitation room. During the hour, my brother had to stand in a line of prisoners and each of them had to be stripped-searched. Some guards limited how long we could visit, while others did not. So, we never knew how long the visits would last.

I have also learned from my brother, what solitary confinement and lockdowns are. Solitary confinement is where they place an inmate in a separate cell, in a different part of the prison. Isn't being in prison enough? In solitary confinement, you are left alone in a cell for 23 hours a day. Lockdown is similar but there is no isolation. In these cases, all the inmates are in their cells for 23 hours a day. During solitary confinement and lockdown, I could not visit or talk to my brother. Sometimes we traveled to the prison and found out when we got there it was a lockdown.

Talking to my brother on the phone was challenging because of the cost. He could only make collect calls and those calls were expensive. The calls were recorded and limited to 15 minutes. Several years later, the system allowed inmates to email. Again, there was a cost to send the email, and a cost to receive the email. Though I don't see my brother that often, we have a strong bond.

The following is a note from my brother and life from his perspective:

I grew up on the far south side of Chicago in what was called the wild hundreds on 122nd and State Street. Both of my parents were present at home, married. I, along with my two sisters, one, three years older and one three years younger. We all were adopted incredibly early in our lives. I have no brothers. I remember when my younger sister, Valerie, was brought home. She was dressed in a green onesie and placed on the floor upon a blanket behind where my older sister and I sat watching television. I reckon a lot could be said about those early years, but besides a few scattered and chaotic memories, I can't truly recall much of them. My younger sister was often sick with asthma, and I recall always feeling some concern about that without really understanding why.

My Father was a large man with a deep resounding voice and a demeanor that did not allow for disobedience or disrespect. I recall my Mother as well as a source of comfort in an otherwise uncomfortable place. I believe my parents did the best they could. I never felt as if I belonged or fit into the family. I remember once Mom and my sisters were tickling my Father, but I was too scared to join in. My Mom noticed and commented on it, and I remember thinking and feeling as if I still didn't belong. My elder sister was very mean-spirited and spiteful, and she used my fear of our Father to control and dominate me. She made my life a living hell. I suspect she herself suffered from some form of abuse, and I bore the brunt of her anger and rage.

Not only did I not defend myself against the anger resentments of our older sister, I also didn't protect Valerie from it either. I guess I was being selfish and honestly relieved the focus wasn't on me. However, there were brief moments, I would join in with her. As she taunted and teased Valerie, I never stopped to think how Valerie thought or felt about it. I figured she was all right. I could not see past my own troubles at the time. Plus, I knew my Father did not punish Valerie as he would punish me and my older sister. In my mind, she was safe.

I can remember how our parents made a big deal of our grades. At first, I made A's and B's just as Valerie so at the beginning of my eighth-grade year, I remember the next semester asking how I'd went from A's to F's. I always saw Val as independent and strong-willed. If she wanted it, she got it. No matter what or how long it took, she was indeed good at persuading our Father to do as she asked or wanted.

I wasn't much of an older brother to her. I feared I had no one to show or teach me how. I was not brave so at the times I ought to have stepped up and shielded her, I ducked and ran for myself. As we grew older, I just figured she was fine. She was smart and outgoing, made excellent grades in school and had many friends. It was not until many years later, in my mid-thirties, I came to understand what my failure as a big brother created for and within her. I went to prison at 16, so that didn't leave much time for "reflection".

During a time period of only being out a few months, I abruptly moved out of the family home. Once again, I concentrated on and only saw my own hurts, issues, wants, and needs. It wasn't until I was in therapy in prison, I came to understand how my abrupt departures had affected Valerie. Now, I always see her as my goddess. She was the only good and kind person in my life. The one who did not judge or condemn me, the only one who accepted and loved me for who I am. In later years as I transitioned to the prison world, often it's been Val, who has kept me grounded. It was at her suggestion I enrolled in therapy and participated fully, in which I ultimately completed a full therapy program while in prison.

Without her, her words of encouragement, advice, and love ... without her support, both emotionally and financially, my time in prison would have been vastly different, definitely harder without her. I doubt if I would be the person, I am today. So yeah, instead of the big brother guiding, nurturing, and protecting my younger sister, it's been Val who has guided nurtured, and protected me. She has always been a unique and phenomenal person. She is Valerie Renee.

~NICHOLAS PETERSON

America's criminal justice system is broken. It can take several years to get a court date and most of the time, there was a continuation because either the State or Defense was unprepared. The system is set up for failure, not success.

In December of 2017, my brother had a release date. This release date allowed my brother to be discharged and placed on parole. For that to happen, my brother had to go before a panel that would decide whether or not he could come home. In order to be released, my brother would have had to have an approved place to live and work. For individuals with felonies such as my brother, this is challenging for the inmate, and their families.

Approved housing for my brother required him to have no internet access or cell phone. He would have had to register in the offender registry and pay an annual registration fee for the rest of his life. He would have had to submit DNA for another registry. He would be on house arrest and could not leave without the approval of his parole officer. This created a new set of obstacles that could become difficult to overcome. My brother has been incarcerated for over 20 years. The technological advances alone could make it difficult for him to adjust in society. He only knows the outside world before he was imprisoned since the 90's. My brother does not know how many functions were added to a cell phone.

As family, we were ready to support my brother. We bought new bedding and new clothes to welcome him home. Together we helped him locate medical care and work. Unfortunately, the parole board opted not to approve his parole. He remained in custody after serving 80% of his time. He was sent back to finish the 20% left on his sentence. As he reached the milestone of serving 100% of his time, I started preparing for his discharge. I was excited to pick my brother up from the prison and drive him home to Chicago. I scheduled flights to meet him and created an itinerary to welcome him home. My Mother prepared dinner of his favorite foods. He was excited to see our parents and other family members. He wanted to have a second chance though he didn't really have a first chance. My brother was ready to begin again.

The day my brother was to come home, I got a phone call from the prison. I was told I could not pick my brother up. There was no additional information they could give me. I could only wait until his phone call and there was no idea of when that would be. I cancelled my flight and broke the news to my family. We were devastated. I anxiously awaited his call which came a week later. My brother explained that he was turned around. There is an Illinois law that allows him to be detained. Released from the Illinois Department of Corrections, my brother was committed to a mental health facility with the Illinois Department of Public Health. To get released, he would face a new court trial. To me, this is double jeopardy.

My brother was being prosecuted again by the state and would have to go through a new trial to fight for his freedom. Every crime my brother committed in the Juvenile Justice Center would be at play to determine if he posed a risk to society.

This was confusing and difficult to understand. My brother completed 100% of his original sentence and exceled at every program the prison required him to enter. He had a favorable rating from his therapist and the prison. He was ticket free for over ten years which meant that he did not get in any trouble. He also completed credentials for horticulture, horse rearing welding, and psychology.

My brother is still in custody by the Illinois Department of Public Health. All of this time has been spent going in and out of the courts to receive a trial date. The trial date continues to come and go. At the time of this writing, my brother's trial has not started. Prisons are supposed to be places of rehabilitation. The current system in place is not rehabilitation, it is degradation. My brother is strong and resilient. Facing obstacles that are too numerous to count. Trying to help him, I reached out to the American Civil Liberties Union (ACLU) for assistance and the Illinois Governor's office. Here is the response I received from the ACLU.

Dear Ms. Peterson,

Thank you for contacting the ACLU of Illinois about your brother's detention beyond his mandatory supervised release date. We agree with

you that this 'turnaround' or 'violation at the door'
policy is very unfair and possibly unconstitutional.
Unfortunately, the court cases that have been
bought to challenge this practice have so far been
unsuccessful. We and other organizations are
finding out new ways to bring court cases on this
issue. This will take some time; however, we can't
offer any immediate assistance.

I did not hear back from the Governor's office. This process is difficult, yet my brother looks forward to being home one day soon. He wants to live in the middle of nowhere and be a farmer. That brings him peace, and I know someday I will be able to visit him and sit on his porch.

THE CHURCH

Most of my youth, outside of school, was spent in church. Prayer meeting on Monday. Choir rehearsal on Tuesday. Bible Study on Wednesday. More choir rehearsal on Thursday, and a testimony service on Friday more like a pep rally than church as folks told the congregation just how good God had been to them. On Saturdays at home, we cleaned to the smooth voice of Herb Kent, the cool Gent from V-103 in Chicago. Often times, I spent Saturdays watching my Mom and Dad clean cases of chicken at church because they were both cooks of the church, and on Sunday, we had church services.

I grew up in an Apostolic Pentecostal church without knowing Apostolic and Pentecostal were different denominations. I was saved, sanctified, Holy Ghost-filled, and water baptized in 'Jesus's name'. I knew how to speak in tongues, but I can honestly say the spirit of God was not allowing me to communicate with him directly, I was simply mimicking others.

I was in the tarrying room frequently. This is the room where we tarry for the gift of the Holy Ghost. It was a session where I would repeat the words the altar workers, people in the church who help you find your way, told me that included Jesus and Hallelujah. Now that I think about it, anytime you say the words 'Jesus' or 'Hallelujah' extremely fast, you will get tongue tied and start creating words you have never spoken before. It was part of my foundation, and I would never deny my experience. In my matureness, I have witnessed the power of God for myself.

Our church believed in water baptism. Baptism represents the close of a previous life and the birth of a new one. I was baptized at a young age. I didn't know why; I just knew that I was taught that I needed to complete this in order to go to Heaven. Since I was aware, I did not want to burn in hell, I did what I was told.

I did not just attend church, I was involved. I sang alto in the choir until one day I was told to move to the soprano side of the choir stand. I worked in the kitchen helping my parents cook for the members. I was an Usher. I did everything I could to make sure my name would be in the 'Lamb's Book of Life' (Revelation 20:15 emphasis added) as we were taught. I was taught to be on fire for God and I knew how that was supposed to look. I was taught I had to live within God's will. If I did not, I would be damned to a hell which they say is seven times hotter than the earth could ever get. I remember times I would be in 'sin'. I would wonder if the trumpets would sound, and Heaven's gates would open would I be condemned to hell? In other words, left behind.

I am proud of the religious upbringing I had. It gave me a moral and ethical foundation. I cannot deny my foundation but when you mature, it's okay to question things you were taught. As I grew older, I questioned a lot of those teachings. I wondered why wearing red lipstick was a sin. Why did wearing a skirt above my knee make me *hussy*? More importantly, why would a God who loves me, a God who knew me before he formed me in the womb damn me to a place called hell because of my outer appearance?

Based on my life, I've been to hell, stayed in hell, and been beneath hell without knowing how to get out. Getting to the other side of tough times feels heavenly. Each time you arise from a pit the heavens open, and you become awake and begin anew. The sun shines brighter. I now know the church I attended was not the only church with access to God. The pastor, prophets, and preachers were not the only people who could go to God on your behalf. You can go to God yourself and you're the only one who can dictate what your individual relationship with God means. No one can define that on your behalf because it's your relationship.

At the very foundation of our being is the choice to know God and to know Him for ourselves. It doesn't matter what you call this higher power but knowing this is what will help you navigate this journey we all call life.

As long as you know God for yourself, you're free to get to know Him better in the way which works for you.

There are many paths to 'believing' in God but with knowing, the path is straight and narrow and there is freedom in understanding.

I **KNOW** there is a God, a higher power, something in the universe to guide you, that takes care of you and knows the why of everything that happens in life. I have felt God's warmth, experienced God's love, and I fellowship with God daily which is how I receive information and guidance. Now don't get me wrong, there have been many times where I wondered where God was or questioned why God placed me in a specific situation. But what I have learned is the beauty of knowing God is in the breakdown. Anytime you have a crisis and I have had many, it's an opportunity to stop, breathe, and look within. There is a scripture in the Old Testament we hear often. This scripture is the foundation for this book.

For I KNOW the thoughts I think toward you, saith the Lord, thoughts of peace and not of evil, to give you an expected end.

Jeremiah 29:11
(KJV – King James Version)

For I KNOW the plans I have for you, declares the LORD, plans to prosper you and not to harm you, plans to give you hope and a future.

Jeremiah 29:11
(NIV – New International Version)

This is GOD's Word on the subject: "As soon as Babylon's seventy years are up and not a day before, I'll show up and take care of you as I promised and bring you back home. I know what I'm doing. I have it all planned out—plans to take care of you, not abandon you, plans to give you the future you hope for.

Jeremiah 29:10-11
(MSG – The Message)

As a single voice, we can take the literal interpretation and continue moving on with our lives thinking there will always be peace and every experience will be a good one. We can also look at the verse in context and learn even more. In looking at the context, this message was given to oppressed people who wanted to give up.

Knowing God means you understand how to communicate with God. This communication happens through prayer and meditation. Prayer and meditation are different. For me, Prayer is a conversation with God. It's our opportunity to give thanks for all of the things God has done, and it's our opportunity to ask God to bless us with things we think we need. Meditation is where we get answers to the questions we have. When we silence our minds, we get the wisdom and the guidance to move forward. In meditation you are present in the moment and basking in the presence of a God.

When you meditate, you quiet your mind. You're not thinking or creating. You're listening. You're open and receptive to guidance. Mediation is a skill you have to learn and practice. I'm still not fully there, but I continue to find time for myself to settle down and be quiet. Many times, I still have all kinds of thoughts in my head about what I want to do and what I need to do. The key is to capture all of those thoughts and to renounce inconsequential thoughts. For example, when I am in mediation, all the menial thoughts come to mind – what I am going to eat, what am I going to wear tomorrow, what shoes will go with my outfit?

I have also learned how to separate religion and spirituality. As I have grown in my spirituality, I have learned about different spiritual tools that helped me significantly. To the church I grew up in, this was considered witchcraft and sorcery in the mainstream Pentecostal church. This is where fear of going to hell would keep me from learning about these things:

- Metaphysics: Metaphysics is the study of the human mind. It allows you to think on a higher level about who you are as an individual. It helped me understand that I am one with God. Metaphysics welcomes everyone. It's not a religious doctrine. You can still have your own beliefs. If something doesn't speak to you, you can throw it away. The goal is to help you strengthen your relationship with God's Spirit ... and not the way others define God for you.

- Healing via Healers: A healer is a person who is intuitive or an empath. From my experience, they can see what you cannot see and tell you with precision what has happened in your life and what the next steps need to be. In the church I grew up in, this is defined as discernment or the gift of knowledge. When I first experienced healers, I learned a different meaning for the word prophecy. In church there are false prophets that promise more material things than spiritual growth. The Biblical perspective is more of a word from God for guidance. I left the healing session wondering. "How is it a person that doesn't know me tell me about my life?" I leave healers with answers, feeling uplifted. For me, this is not demonic. This is spiritual. This is based on my experience.

- Crystals Healing: I love the healing energy of crystals. I learned about crystals from one of my healing sessions. It piqued my interest and I sought to learn more about them and their use. There are crystals that amplify the intentions you have. Crystals are natural and come from the earth. They function as another tool that helps with balance, removing negative energy and living a life of desire versus a life of lack.

- Sound: Most people enjoy music but don't really understand sound. Sound has vibrations. Sound healing can be accompanied by crystal bowls, Tibetan singing bowls as well as tuning forks and Solfeggio frequencies which are tones that can relax and strengthen you.

Knowing I am one with God and God is one with me, is liberating. Information is one of the most valuable tools we can have. With new information, you can do different things and also change your mind which brings freedom.

There are so many religions and different practices, but they all lead to God. We are using different routes to get there. Who are we to say what is right or what is wrong.

How do you define God?

_____

_____

_____

_____

_____

_____

_____

_____

_____

_____

_____

_____

_____

_____

_____

_____

_____

THE HEALING CRISIS

We Wear the Mask

Poem by:
~**PAUL LAURENCE DUNBAR**

We wear the mask that grins and lies,

It hides our cheeks and shades our eyes, —

This debt we pay to human guile;

With torn and bleeding hearts we smile,

And mouth with myriad subtleties.

Why should the world be over-wise,

In counting all our tears and sighs?

Nay, let them only see us, while

We wear the mask.

We smile, but, O great Christ, our cries

To thee from tortured souls arise.

We sing, but oh the clay is vile

Beneath our feet, and long the mile;

But let the world think otherwise,

We wear the mask!

*   *   *

Take the mask off! A lie will only last until the truth arrives! People love my smile. My cheekbones, my eyes, and my teeth. I love my smile too but it's a coverup a lot of times. No one can see behind my smile except me.

A "healing crisis" is a medical condition in which your body becomes overwhelmed and literally has to remove everything toxic. Sometimes, nature forces out the toxins. Other times, only medical intervention can rid your body of its toxicity.

Your mental and emotional states must be cleansed, so you can become whole again. If you don't get rid of the toxins, your body starts breaking down. Externally, you might lose your hair, have brittle nails, and internally brain fog, digestive issues, or headaches.

Internally, the blood supplies nutrients to your body and the cells fight to keep you well are in overtime trying to combat the foreign enemies. Until you can recognize the war raging inside your body, you cannot heal. Yes, you can ignore it, wish it away, pray it away or use some other system. But until you acknowledge you're sick and hurting, your mind and body will begin to breakdown. I was tired of being broken, and I knew I had to be healed.

It sounds easy. It's almost like you can flip a switch and be healed. Unfortunately, it does not work like that. You must make a mental and emotional determination that you want and deserve to be healed. Do that, and the choice lies within. It takes a hell of a lot of work to be free, and rest assured you're never alone. Help is always here and it's always near.

When I look in the mirror, I see a person that has a lot of hurt and pain. I see a person that has turmoil brewing inside that I'm afraid to confront. People see me as a happy go lucky easy-going person who is full of life, but yet, I see myself as dull and lifeless at times with the potential for greatness. What people don't see is the internal struggle with the dark side of myself. I don't like the person I see in the mirror. She fronts a lot because she doesn't know who she is. She pretends to be what she is not.

~VALERIE

What mask are you wearing that you need to take off?

_____
_____
_____
_____
_____
_____
_____
_____
_____
_____
_____
_____
_____
_____
_____
_____
_____
_____
_____
_____
_____
_____
_____
_____

THREE WORDS
"I NEED HELP"

This doesn't work for me anymore. I'm suffering. I have lost my mind. This was not supposed to happen to me. Not Miss Super Strong Valerie. How did I end up here? How did I end up in a drunken stupor and cycle of weed, eat, drink, sleep ... weed, eat, drink, sleep?

~VALERIE

People look at me and see somebody who's a strong, courageous, independent black woman. I always looked like I had everything together and in public, I did. Sharp. Sassy. Intelligent. Various people in my life have a puzzle piece. Only a few know the whole story. Life has a way of bringing out what is hidden inside.

Grief stings. One moment a person is here, and the next moment they're not.

My Father was diagnosed with the Coronavirus (COVID-19) at the beginning of the pandemic. During this time, there was not much known. I learned about COVID-19 by watching news sources that are overseas. Having a background in Community Health enabled me to quickly assess the trajectory of its rapid infection rates and death rates. We knew it was a contagious virus that caused pneumonia. Treatment for COVID-19 was sporadic; research on how to treat it was also lacking. Intuitively, I began to feel uneasy about the path of the virus and began ordering medical care items and other necessities in January. I shipped some to me, and I shipped some to my parents. At first, they thought I was a bit crazy. Soon after, news reported the virus was in the United States, this is when I got nervous.

My Dad suffered from several health conditions that impacted the way COVID-19 interacted in his body. This includes diabetes and chronic heart failure. My Dad was a compassionate man. He did not let the virus change his day-to-day living. I admire that in spite of it, he kept moving forward serving providing the needs of others in the community and in the church.

The week before my Dad went to the hospital, I could tell he was not feeling well. Every day I called him to check on him. After telling me he was fine, I sent a friend of mine to the house to check on him. Like me, my sister, also wanted to make sure that he had items to take care of his sickness. After urging my Father to go to the hospital, he was admitted on April 3, 2020. My Dad did not like hospitals so trying to get him there was a task my sister took on quickly. She could not walk into the ER. She dropped him off at the door. He was left in the hands of the doctors.

I spoke to my dad several times while he was hospitalized. On the first call I knew he was having difficulty breathing. I told him to get some rest and that I would text him later. I told him I loved him on the phone and then I sent it through a text message. On April 9, 2020, I talked to my Dad. He said he was getting better and that he was resting. He assured me he would be home soon. Again, I told him I loved him on the phone, and I said I love you through a text message. I realize he knows but wanted him to hear it over and over from me.

The morning of April 10, my Mom called the hospital to check in with the nurses. After being placed on the phone for a long while, the nurse came back to the phone. She shared that everything was going well for my Dad. He had asked the nurses to turn off his light so he could sleep. After the nurses left, my Dad went into cardiac arrest. At 7:15 a.m. on April 10, my Dad passed away.

I received word while I was home in Texas with my daughters, my Dad was gone. I felt the phone ringing before it rung. My world stopped. The switch flipped, and I went into care-mode for my daughters. We wept together for hours. Not being able to be in Chicago with my Mother and sister was devastating. When my Mother and my sister went to get my Dad's personal belongings, my Mother called to tell me what was on his cellphone. It was a picture of a hand stretching out from the clouds. The text read, 'soon and very soon'. It became clear to me that my dad was ready to die. In a sense, he was at peace with life. He was ready to go. My Dad spoke of dying to the point we would roll our eyes after hearing him say it so many times.

I am thankful for my sister. Though we've had tension in our relationship, she stepped up to be there for my Mom to make all the funeral arrangements, to view the body, and the clothing my dad would wear. Funeral homes were back logged due to the excessive number of deaths in the State. It was not until April 22 that my Dad was able to have a funeral. Only ten people could attend the funeral and the burial. My daughters and I were unable to be there in person. It was hard for me to view my Dad's body through a cell phone. I opted not to watch the funeral. It was surreal that my Dad was on a screen in a casket. The last time I saw him in person was on New Year's Day 2020, the day of my sister's wedding.

After my dad's death, I was laying at the bottom of a rabbit hole, crying out from the abyss. I knew I had to get up. I knew I could not stay there because if I stayed there, I would have died. I would have killed myself to free myself from an unbearable pain. I did not want to die. Instead, I recognized I needed help.

As Iyanla Vanzant prays, I prayed. "Help me, Help me now! Please. Thank you!"

Death can be the greatest teacher. Sometimes it takes pain to change the trajectory of your life. Whether it's a physical death of a loved one or the representative death of something that mattered to you like a relationship, a job, a long-winded bad habit, etc.

There is no stigma attached to needing help. The only stigma is the one you assign yourself. You have to get to the point. You are the most important person in your life. Often, we seek out others who share the same pain because we want to feel like we are not alone, which can lead down a road of destruction. Recognizing you need help is one of the best and most fulfilling things you can do for yourself. I was brave enough to get help, now I am brave enough to tell the story.

When I ask for help, I have learned to never reject it especially when someone is willing to help. There were times I felt unworthy and would question someone's true intentions or motives. Well regardless, when people want to help, I must be willing to receive their help. I could hear the words in my mind, *get to work*. You have to learn how to move forward.

Dear God, please take all of the situations in my life that cause me to weep, be anxious, and to fear the worst-case scenario. I want to learn how to stay present and acknowledge the gifts I have right now. Help me learn how to navigate this journey because only the experiences you give me, can make me stronger. I must get rid of my ego and the junk to create more space for your presence and your love. Teach me God, to learn how to ask for help so I can be in a position to love and to create space for those who need me and that you will draw me to you. I'm ready.

What do you need help with right now?

_____
_____
_____
_____
_____
_____
_____

Who can you reach out to for support?

_____
_____
_____
_____
_____
_____
_____

How would you feel if this problem was resolved?

_____
_____
_____
_____
_____
_____
_____

THIS IS YOUR FAULT

When I was 13 years old, my circle was small outside of church. I shared a close bond with the friends that I did have. My friends and I always had fun. I felt like I was a member of the family. Not only did I interact with their immediate family, but I also interacted with their extended family. We felt like brothers, sisters, and cousins.

One time I was at a friend's house, which was nothing new, we were having so much fun, I decided to spend the night. I always spent time with my best friend, her cousins, and neighbors. We stayed up pretty late telling plenty of jokes, playing card games, board games, pillow fights, watching movies, and outside play.

Tired from the activities of the day, it was time for me to go to sleep. My mouth was dry, so I went to get a drink of water. My favorite is cold ice water. I opened the refrigerator door and leaned over to get the water and was approached by one of my friends' cousins. Initially, I was startled. Then it became clear, her cousin was drunk or high. He pushed me down a flight of stairs located on the side of the refrigerator that led into the basement. I was ordered down the stairs with force. I was told to keep my mouth shut. I started getting scared because this was not his normal behavior. When he pushed me, I fell hitting the bottom of the staircase hard then stood quickly to get away. He then pushed me down and started forcing sex on me, covering my mouth so no one could hear my screams.

I did not know what was going on. All I felt was a sharp, stabbing pain in my abdomen unlike anything I had ever experienced. When he finished, he removed his hand from my mouth and warned me not to share what happened with anyone. I ran to the bathroom to shower. When the water started, I noticed a trickle of blood between my legs. Still, it did not register that I had been raped. When I returned to the room, my friend was sound asleep, I tapped her on the shoulder and asked her for some feminine pads. Then I told her what her cousin had done. She blamed me and told me it was my fault.

With so many thoughts running through my head, I was baffled by my best friend saying it was my fault. I was responsible for being raped by her cousin. Over and over, I replayed the moment in my mind. Each time, I pondered my actions. I never figured out what I did to cause it. After that, I held that belief. I did not share it until 25 years later.

I finally determined it was not my fault when I shared my story with another close friend. He accompanied me to share my story with a group of high school girls speaking about the rape and how it fit into my life. After hearing me speak, he told me the rape was not my fault. I stopped dead in my tracks. I had never heard that before. Now, it was my time to let go and heal. Part of healing was to contact my best friend from childhood. I wanted her to know how it made me feel when she blamed me. When I eventually told her, she apologized. She did not remember much about the incident but insisted she would have reacted differently if she had been older.

I finally released the anger I did not even know I had. Rape is sometimes buried deep into our essence. It becomes a part of us, and it affects us years after the actual act occurs. It's unforgettable. That's why we must learn to speak out and support each other. Each experience makes us the person we become. It's hard when you have had a traumatic experience to make sense of it, but better is the end of the thing than the beginning thereof. In the pain, we can find strength.

It was not my fault. It was never my fault. For rape victims, silence is the easier reaction. We can feel ashamed and dirty and think we can get over it ourselves. We lose our sense of self. Sharing our story with a trusted friend or therapist can help us to release. Many people have been affected by rape. We share in this pain, but silence should no longer be an option. This was an experience that we could not control. It's time to free ourselves and share our story.

RAPE TRAUMA SYNDROME

Rape Trauma Syndrome is a condition only few people know. It's one of many symptoms that occurs after sexual violence, which includes psychological trauma. This condition has three primary phases: acute, outward adjustment, and resolution.

The Acute phase occurs right after the sexual violence has occurred. Outward adjustment happens when the victim tries to function normally, and the resolution phase begins when the sexual violence is no longer part of your life.

After my rape, I became silent. Being told it was my fault played a key role in my inability to share my story with anyone else. I kept it to myself. It took me more than 20 years to discuss the rape with a therapist, who informed me about Rape Trauma Syndrome. I realized the rape led to many of the psychological conditions I struggled to manage. Research conducted by the Rape and Incest National Network (www.rainn.org) show the side effects of rape trauma which includes:

- Anxiety: One of the conditions I still struggle with today.
- Severe Mood Swings: This confirms the diagnosis of Bipolar 2.
- Sense of Helplessness: I couldn't escape the victim mindset.
- Persistent Fear or Phobia: Included in the anxiety category as I often think about the worst-case scenario in which there is no evidence to support it.
- Depression: The first component I discovered along with the anxiety.
- Eating Difficulties: Overeating, which led to me being morbidly obese.
- Denial or Withdrawal of Friends: Unable to become close to others and abandoning those wanting to support me.
- Difficulty Sleeping: Suffering from Insomnia
- Sexual problems: I became promiscuous three years later.

I am now in the resolution phase. I can share my story from a healthier place versus when I shared it before I was healed. I resolved the rape was not my fault, which took a tremendous amount of courage.

If you or someone you know has experienced sexual violence, The Rape and Incest National Network is available to support you. You can contact them at 1-800-656-HOPE (4673)

TRAUMA AND COPING

Each time a person stands up for an idea or acts to improve the life of others, they send forth a ripple of hope.... These ripples build a current which can sweep down the mightiest walls of oppression and resistance.

~JOHN F. KENNEDY

The pain of our present and our past prepares us for the promises of the present and the future. Pain has no limits, no boundaries, and is not tied to a clock. Neither physical pain nor psychological pain feels good. Both can affect one's ability to function properly.

I have a dog named Logan, a *Pomsky*, who serves as my emotional support dog. My therapist suggested I buy him. I speak more about Logan in the Emotion Rehabilitation Compassion and Self-Care chapter in this book. I also have another dog, a Puggle named Bentley. Bentley is my daughter's emotional support dog. Bentley is the 'OG', and Logan is the spoiled brat like I was.

Bentley and Logan have mixed feelings about each other. Some days, they get along; other times they don't. One day Logan and Bentley were playing, and they started fighting. Bentley bit Logan that caused him to require stitches. To this day, Logan licks the wound even though the fight was more than three years ago.

According to the Animal Kennel Club, a dog's saliva contains antibacterial properties. When the wound is fresh, the dog uses its tongue to help heal themselves. As long as the dog does not excessively lick the wound when it's fresh, it will heal faster.

Trauma takes years to overcome. You can have flashbacks and nightmares about a traumatic experience for years. Logan licking his wounds proves he has not forgotten the fight. There is further information on Logan later in the book.

People use the term 'lick your wounds' to signal someone to forget their trauma or pain and move on. This is easier said than done. Traumatic experiences are buried deep in the conscious and subconscious mind. As much as we want to forget, we cannot. The key is to ask for help, so you can receive support.

Based on my experience with Post Traumatic Stress Disorder (PTSD), people sense your trauma. You know the saying, "misery loves company". There is a lot of truth in it, but we must protect ourselves from ourselves. I did that very thing by:

1. Making time for the quiet space,

2. Reducing chaos and clutter from my home, and
3. Remembering that I matter.

Many of us see ourselves as victims with little capacity to recognize we shape and determine what happens next through the decisions we make. Healing takes place as we speak and live our own truth.

Mindfulness challenges us to consciously stay in the present moment. We must be aware of the thoughts we have. Are the thoughts we allow to play in our minds positive or negative? How does the body feel? What is around us? How are we feeling? Is there anything we need at the moment? Being mindful also helps us respond to people differently. We can be fully present in conversation and day-to-day activities. Mindfulness was difficult for me in the beginning. I would try to not have negative thoughts, but the more I did, the more negative thoughts I had. Some were positive and most were negative. I had to learn how to catch the negative thoughts and replace them with positive thoughts and try to reach for the gap between the two thoughts to become centered.

Yoga helped me to become mindful. It provided a space for me to learn how to be in the present moment. It also allows for stretching which benefits the physical body. With yoga, I had to get to the place where I did not care about how I looked while I was doing poses which is easy to do when you are surrounded by people who are yoga pros. I also learned about my stopping point. The point at which I try to push forward and try a specific pose. If it becomes too much, I modify the pose or use moments for rest. When I do stop to rest, I examine how I am feeling and the thoughts I have.

What traumatic experience have you had in your life?

_____
_____
_____
_____
_____
_____
_____
_____
_____
_____

What are your feelings regarding this trauma you wrote about?

_____
_____
_____
_____
_____
_____
_____
_____
_____
_____

How do you picture your life without this trauma?

_____
_____
_____
_____

_____
_____
_____
_____
_____
_____
_____

What are your plans moving forward?

_____
_____
_____
_____
_____
_____
_____
_____
_____
_____

What technique do you use to quiet your mind?

_____
_____
_____
_____
_____
_____
_____
_____
_____
_____

COPING

When you cope with something, you're dealing with a stressful situation. There is a fine line between coping with something in a healthy manner versus going down a rabbit hole. Coping can cause learned helplessness. Coping requires action based on the right now.

You either have healthy or unhealthy ways to cope. I coped by drinking obsessively, smoking marijuana heavily, and sleeping. This is the rabbit hole. What I wanted was a place to escape. I did not want to feel the effects of the situation. I felt like it would be too much to handle. I wanted to be left alone. To escape the rabbit hole, I had to seek support from someone I trust.

If you cannot be honest with yourself, how can you be honest with someone else? Acknowledging what you need takes you from the rabbit hole and points you toward healing. Sometimes, it takes a couple of days, a couple of weeks or in my case, months. I had to slow down on the dope and learn to cope. Once you admit you're in a bad place, you can create an action plan with goals that leads to healing and restoration. Once you enter the rabbit hole, it's easy to stay there. It's easy to make others feel bad for you.

I am sure we have seen posts on social media that goes something like this: "Pray for me, no questions, just pray." I have posted this message several times to quench the thirst of attention. I needed to be fed sympathy, so I could stay where I was. It took away my personal accountability and I thought I was happy not caring.

Healthy coping skills require effort. A friend of mine who is a school counselor says that you have 24 – 48 hours to feel sorry for yourself. After that, you should get up and keep moving forward with a new plan. This becomes easier if you have some skills to help you get up.

What is your coping mechanism?

_____

_____

_____

_____

_____

_____

_____

_____

_____

_____

_____

_____

DEPRESSION

I have so much to be thankful for. Yet, feelings of depression, anxiety and not feeling good enough always seems to overtake me. I know I am a beautiful woman inside and out but how come it's hard to own. Part of it is I don't want to believe. If you were to ask me why, I don't have an answer. What I do know for sure is I am special and favored by God.

~VALERIE

Life is precious and fragile. From physical health to mental health to emotional health, things can quickly go downhill. Depression is real. There is a deep physical, indescribable pain associated with it. It's more than losing interest in things, it's more than feeling sad. It physically hurts. Alongside the physical pain, there is the emotional pain. Guilt, shame, and insecurity. Any negative word you can think of, describes the feeling. Anxiety is not any better. Uncontrollable thoughts, always expecting the worst-case scenario, listening to your heart race, and feeling the sweat running down your face is exhausting. Being constantly consumed with fear and panic of the unknown is torturous.

Depression is real. I am not talking about being sad, being down. I am speaking about depression. Not wanting to get up and shower because you have no energy and don't want to go anywhere. The lack of energy to put toothpaste on a toothbrush and brush your teeth. Lying in bed with tons of weight on your back is the type of depression I am talking about, and I have experienced over half of my life.

The physical pain manifests itself in many ways. For me, it sometimes feels like a knot is stuck in the middle of my throat. Chest pain and congestion that is really not there but is there. This is the time where phone calls don't get answered, e-mails and voicemails get no response. It's a time to disappear from the world I perceive is bringing physical pain.

Anxiety is depression's sidekick. The moments when your thoughts take you to places you never deemed imaginable, your heart beats, sweat runs down your face, and the pressing fear that something bad is going to happen is a panic attack. Anxiety also has a feeling associated with it that is indescribable. Tickles in the hands, stomach, and a slight headache.

I have suffered from depression and anxiety for more than twenty years. I was first diagnosed after the birth of my second daughter. I have also been diagnosed with Bipolar 2 Disorder, Borderline Personality Disorder, and Post Traumatic Stress Disorder (PTSD). I have had a cocktail of medications which include me being on the following medications at some point through my mental health journey. I have been on Prozac, Abilify, Trazadone, Lamictal, Serzone, Wellbutrin, Klonopin, Zoloft and Buspar. Because Insomnia goes along with, I can include being on, Temazepam, Ambien, Sonata and Gabapentin. Now I know this sounds like a lot, and it is. Most of the time my psychiatrists were trying to find the right drug and combinations to get me to a therapeutic dose.

The majority of these medications have side effects. Most of the times they were not great. Weird dreams, ringing in the ears, rapid heartbeats, feeling like I wanted to jump out my skin and other feelings I cannot explain. It's pretty bad when a doctor says you may need to be on a medication forever as I was told, but I learned there was no truth in that of a false belief I accepted.

The new awareness is recognizing I am falling into the pit of depression and anxiety is beginning to take over my life. Step one is the recognition of realizing you're in trouble. I know myself better than anyone, just like you know yourself better than anyone. I have learned to recognize and know when I need to seek additional help. This is not a weakness, it's a superpower. The ability to know when you are in trouble and can gather enough energy and strength to make a phone call and say, "I need ... Help!" This is not something you get to overnight. Like everything else, it's a process. A piece of process is already having a support system of people and things that help usher you back to the place where the road is sunny regardless if you see the sun or not.

Transitions are triggers for my depression. Going to school shielded me from feeling depression. I did not even know I was depressed until I shared my feelings and symptoms with a doctor. I knew something was not right, and I wanted to change. Stress + depression + anxiety are a bad combination for me.

Depression/anxiety requires a tremendously strong person to endure its pain. You are that person. It may not feel like it, but you are.

~THE ANXIETY MAN

If you've experienced depression, how have you coped?

_____

_____

_____

_____

_____

_____

_____

_____

_____

_____

HEALING BROKENNESS

*I wish to live because life has within it that which is good,
which is beautiful, and that which is love. Therefore, since
I have known all these things, I have found them to be
reason enough and I wish to live. Moreover, because this
is so, I wish others to live for generations and generations
and generations and generations.*

~**LORRAINE HANSBERRY**

Many of us walk alone ... broken. We carry alongside us the baggage of emotional pain, feelings of betrayal, and very deep sorrows. We sometimes stay silent and suffer alone because we feel like we are the only one. Living like this is to live in a state of constant chaos and the chaos literally kills you from the inside out. For over 25 years, I have struggled with depression, anxiety, borderline personality disorder, post-traumatic stress disorder, high blood pressure, high cholesterol, morbid obesity, and alopecia. The stress was overwhelming. My body broke down which caused me to break down. I hid behind the truth of who I really was. I became exhausted from living in deceit. Yes, I looked strong on the outside, but on the inside, I was dying. I needed to be healed. Healing did not happen and will not happen in one day at one particular time. The only guaranteed fix is death.

Suicide was an option and an option I thought was the only way out. I'd had enough, I could not take the pain away, and I could not figure out what the next step was. In that moment, I thought it was suicide. It was a Saturday night when I decided to commit suicide. I also prayed to God that night. I prayed to God asking what my purpose was in life. I also bargained with God and said if it's not for me to die, wake me up in the morning.

That night I took several drugs including sleeping pills, pain pills, and anti-anxiety meds. After taking these meds, I started crying because now it is too late. I was out of it. I began thinking about my daughters and that their grandparents could take better care of them than I could. I fell asleep and did not realize I was sleeping. When I awoke in the morning feeling extremely drowsy, a different type of energy overcame me which made me get out of bed. It was a Sunday morning, and I needed to go to a place where I could be surrounded by others and that happened to be Church.

I walked through the doors and was greeted with love and hugs as I always was. I sat in service, barely participated but knew it was a good place to be. As church was wrapping up, my pastor at the time stopped the service. He requested it become silent and nobody should leave the sanctuary. This is the moment my energy shifted, and I became extremely anxious. At the moment the Pastor asked everybody to start praying as there was a person in the church who just tried to kill themselves. At the time, I felt like I had disconnected from my body. Somehow, I knew the Pastor was talking about me. He then said to the congregation, "If that's you, come forward." God said you are not done yet. Your healing is here. No one moved as I tried to hide my anxiety. The church began praying. It was like someone had lifted me out of my seat and escorted me to the front of the church even though I walked on my own. At the front, the Pastor as well as a team of prayer warriors, surrounded me in prayer. I had received the answer I prayed about. God said, "You're not done."

I knocked on the door of suicide, and it did not open. I am glad it did not because if it did, I would not be here to share with you the route to heal when you feel like you have nothing left to give. Suicide is not the answer.

My heart has been broken many times, and I am incredibly good at hiding the pain and putting on the mask. A lot of us associate broken hearts with things which happened outside of our control, relationships that did not work out the way we wanted them to, or the loss of someone or something we loved or had an attachment.

Maya Angelou once said, "When a person shows you who they are, believe them **the first time."** Part of the quote is something a lot of us miss out on. The first impression may not always be the most accurate, but by the third or fourth interaction, you should have an idea of what you're dealing with. The moment you rely on someone else, you give up on yourself and the ability you have within to succeed.

Broken hearts and brokenness can be repaired. You just have to do the work. You have to realize there will never be a time where you awake and all of a sudden, your broken heart is mended. To heal a broken heart is to engage in a lengthy process of learning how to love all over again. For me, it was learning how to love Valerie ... yes, learning how to love myself. I carried around a lot of defenses against experiencing feelings. That is why it was so easy to get into the rut of despair ... the "give up" attitude. I had to stop treating myself like a garbage dump and you have to do the same. I had to become more mindful about how I was treating myself and taking care of my body.

I had to ask myself these questions, "Does this support or hurt me? Is this helping my feelings or feeding my feelings?" Sadness and grief were sitting on the surface, and guilt and shame was creating the turmoil inside. I had to get to the place of perfect love which is when I realized I did not do anything wrong; I just needed to navigate the situation differently. I had to find compassion for myself. I had to understand it was healthy to feel the feelings I felt. Becoming aware was my steppingstone to making it to the next day ... every day.

Frustration is not an indication something is wrong with you. Frustration means you may have set your expectations too high. When you are rejected in any way, it just means the person or thing does not have the capacity to operate at the level you're on. As long as you rely on other people to make your life work, you will depend on them. If no one ever gives you an opportunity, create one!

Brokenness brings about change. You can no longer do what broke you, and you cannot be around someone who is broken. Keep positive energy around as much as possible. Keep your vibrations high. Stop hiding behind the pain. Your freedom is here.

In the silence is where I can listen to God's voice, be guided by His intuition, and become aware of the next steps. I'm thankful I'm becoming more comfortable with the silence and also using the silence as a tool to learn about myself.

~VALERIE

If you or someone you know is thinking about or are about to commit suicide, please contact the National Suicide Prevention Lifeline at 800-273-8355. There are healthier ways and support systems to help you get through the dark place in your life.

AFFIRMATIONS

You can't waste time when you have a revelation about who you are and what's in your future. The use of affirmations is a powerful way to speak to yourself.

~VALERIE

Write the vision and make it plain. Say what you heard so you can see what you said. The best way to do this is through affirmations. Affirmations are tools I use to create the reality of who I am and where I want to go. For example, I always had problems with my weight. I did not like the way I looked and the way it felt. When I was honest with myself, I began to change the course of my thinking by using affirmation. No longer would I tell myself I was fat and ugly; I began to affirm I was a beautiful woman with a slender body.

Affirmations allow you to create the things you want in your life. Affirmations should be written in the present tense, so they come to life. Affirmations are also a positive way to change your mindset. I take the most important affirmations and write them on my bathroom mirror with a dry erase marker. I look at it and say it every time I see it. Now, I have written it, so I can see it. This helps me get the message as a fixture in my mind. I also put affirmations on sticky pads and place them in different places in the house. What you focus on expands. So, if you fill your mind with worry and contempt, this will be your reality. If you put into your mind positive things on a consistent basis, your bad habits and negative thinking will slowly fade and one day, it will be a natural habit for you to pull out the good in all situations.

Positive affirmations:
- I love and approve of myself,
- I have a happy slender body,
- I'm in the process of positive change,
- I deserve the best and I accept it now,
- I trust the process of life to bring me my highest good,
- I'm God's child and it's right for me to have love and companionship and fulfillment, and
- I claim it and I give thanks for it.

And then God answered: "Write this. Write what you see. Write it out in big block letters, so that it can be read on the run. This vision-message is a witness pointing to what's coming. It aches for the coming–it can hardly wait! And it doesn't lie. If it seems slow in coming, wait. It's on the way. It will come right on time!

Habakkuk 2:2-3
(MSG - The Message)

RESILIENCE

Leading through pain ... I find it amazing this journal began as a place to document hurt and pain. Now, I'm recognizing the rest of the pages will be filled with the journey to healing and the opportunity to begin again.

Restoration, Renewal, Refocus, Release

~VALERIE

I was in a Gifted Program from preschool until I graduated from high school. This was an accelerated program for students that had a high level of academic success. That success led me to enroll in a high school that doubled as a gifted program after sixth grade. At Kenwood Academy there was an accelerated program. I was able to take high school level courses as an elementary student. There were few students that got admitted to the program, and I was one of them. This was my first time riding a school bus and attending a school that was not in my neighborhood.

Going outside the community I grew up in felt enlightening at first. I had never been exposed to diversity and struggled to fit in. Going to that school was an adjustment for me, and I often acted as the class clown to get attention. There was also an open campus for lunch. An open campus means you can leave if you have an open period and/or on your lunch break. Although, we were served lunch in the lunchroom, we always went out a time or two.

Though there were a lot of support systems to help students become successful, I was not yet skilled on how to talk to teachers. After nearly drowning in a swimming pool because I did not listen in the swim class, to being hit in the head with a rock while on the school bus, to my failing grades, the teachers and administrators knew I did not fit in. I was kicked out.

In high school, I was still the quiet, shy nerdy girl, but then I got introduced to this one boy and fell in love. We spent 90 percent of our time talking on the telephone. The other ten percent of time, I would ditch school to be with him.

My Dad drove the bus route that led to my school. It was funny how I learned his schedule so I could avoid him. It was worth it for my guy. He was the cutest guy ever in my head. He was light-skinned with wavy, curly, beautiful thick hair, and had nice brown eyes with long eyelashes. I gave him my all, in high school. I snuck to talk to him on the phone. We would meet up in different places.

In school, I was smart, and I knew what I wanted to do. After high school, my focus was to study medicine at

Hampton University. I had dreams of becoming a Neonatologist or a Pathologist. No one else in my family attended college. I was determined to be the first one until my junior year of high school, when I found out I was pregnant. Boy, was I shocked! Yes, I never figured out the pullout method wasn't foolproof.

So here I was a 17-year-old pregnant junior in high school. Both of my parents expressed their disappointment. They were sad I would no longer be attending college, even worse, the same teachers who saw me as a smart student wrote me off. From my perspective, my school did not have high expectations for students; there weren't low either. There were no expectations at all. Still, I wanted to go to college. In the midst of all negative energy discouraging me from going to college, one teacher encouraged me and said, "You can go to college, and I'm going to help you." Hearing that gave me a sense of peace because I knew I had support.

When I mentioned the word **COLLEGE**, counselors would laugh at me or try to convince me I should consider dropping out of school to take care of my baby. Every time someone told me what I couldn't do, it made me want to do it. As it got closer to the time for me to have my daughter, I was dismissed from the physical building and homeschooled. Many thought I wouldn't return, but not only did I return to school after I had the baby, I graduated on time.

As a freshman, I didn't know much about class rank or grade point average (GPA). As I learned what each meant, I started to pay more attention to both numbers.

At the end of my freshman year, there was a total of 355 students in our class. By the time I graduated, the number dropped to 110. This was an 'aha' moment for me. Over half of the freshman class, I came in with, was no longer in school. Some transferred, some died, some were incarcerated, and some dropped out. The Chicago public educational system is like many in urban districts where the majority of students are students of color. In some cases, school staff give up on many of us before we even have a chance.

In my search to find a college, I discovered Northern Illinois University had family housing, which meant I could go to college and take my daughter with me. My first semester sucked. It was my first time living alone, which meant I had to work full-time, go to school full-time and take care of my daughter.

When the semester ended, I had a 1.4 GPA, which meant my parents received a letter saying either raise my GPA or get dismissed from the university. I was on academic probation. I did not know I should not schedule classes at 8 a.m. and 7 p.m. on the same day. I had no idea what was going on in math because it was foreign to me. I had never learned it. The review of math concepts alone was enough to give me a headache and to disconnect.

I majored in nursing, which meant the next semester I would have to take higher level courses and retake the chemistry course I failed. All I knew was I needed to improve my grades. I used a strategy my academic advisor did not like. A woman I worked with suggested I take swimming, bowling and first aid to improve my GPA.

I took general education classes which were easier to pass. Thankfully, my GPA increased, and I stayed in school. Things were beginning to go good in my world.

I went to school, worked, studied and took care of my daughter. I also managed to start two hobbies and continue a third one. I had a wonderful, so I thought, new boyfriend who introduced me to weed, alcohol and partying. During the spring semester of the following year, I found out I was pregnant again. Still determined to graduate from college, I had the baby and two weeks later I was taking finals. I have the final say about decisions I make because I am accountable for my actions.

Graduating from college was difficult. I suffered from depression, anxiety, and I don't know how I graduated in four years. One of the things that helped me reach my goal was government assistance. I had food stamps. I had WIC (Woman, Infants, and Children), which supplied baby formula, food, and other staple items. I had daycare assistance and cash assistance which I used to buy diapers. Medicaid covered our doctor's visits and most importantly, I had Section 8 to pay my rent.

You would think I was living a dream life with no effort and dependent on public assistance to live. It wasn't easy being on public assistance. The caseworkers were rude and would procrastinate submitting paperwork. I felt the judgmental energy that made me feel helpless. In my mind, I wanted to do everything I could to get off of it. Using that mindset, I use public assistance to become self-supportive. As I continued in school to get my graduate degree and doctorate, I found a Section 8 Program that helped me buy my first home.

Finally, I found a caseworker who cared. She began walking me through the process of buying a home that included workshop on credit and how to maintain my home. Every time my income increased my rent went up. The difference between the new rent and the old rent was kept in a savings account. After going through home-buying programs and financial-literacy programs, I graduated from Section 8. I used the savings from the program which helped me put a down payment on a condo for me and my daughters on the South Side of Chicago

*   *   *

Resilience is the ability to overcome difficult things. Anytime you overcome obstacles, you take on new knowledge and apply it to your life as you move forward. Here are seven principles of resilience that resonated the most with me from Psychology Today articles by Katherine King Psy.D. I added to it to give my perspective.

Principle 1: Cultivate a Belief in Your Ability to Cope: Affirm you will get through this, even when you don't see the end.

Principle 2: Stay Connected with Sources of Support: Now is not the time to shut down! This is the time to say I need help!

Principle 3: Talk About What You're Going Through: Seek Counseling and go to the appointments … no rescheduling!

Principle 4: Be Helpful to Others: Helping others feel great: It's a confidence booster and you're doing something positive.

Principle 5: Activate Positive Emotion: Affirm and pick out tools from your emotional rehabilitation kit.

Principle 6: Cultivate an Attitude of Survivorship: You survived, you got through it. See yourself as a coach for those who are dealing with similar issues.

Principle 7: Seek Meaning: ask the question 'what did you learn during this time' and answer it with evidence so you can see what helped you get through.

How has resilience shown up in your life?

_____

_____

_____

_____

_____

_____

_____

_____

_____

KNOW WHO YOU ARE

*The fact is, you already know how to find yourself;
you have just gotten distracted and disoriented.
Once refocused, you will realize that you not only
have the ability to find yourself, you have the
ability to free yourself!*

~MICHAEL SINGER

I love Rollercoasters. My Dad took me on my first rollercoaster ride at Six Flags Great America in Gurnee, Illinois. I remember being in line to get on the Whizzer and looking at the ride in anticipation. Waiting in the queue, I was excited about going up the hill and dropping down. I was thrilled about the speed and the twists and the turns. Once it was our time to ride, I carefully sat down and put on the seat belt then my Dad made sure I was secure.

We began zooming around to reach the top of the hill. As we neared the top, I began to get nervous because I did not know what was going to happen next. Five seconds later, we were headed down the hill, twisting, turning, and returning to the station. Finally, we braked. We unbuckled our seatbelts and walked to the next ride.

The rollercoaster is a metaphor for what makes life worth living. All the emotions I felt—anxiety, fear, and excitement—is like working on things to help life become better. This applies to multiple areas. Once we get to the rollercoaster, we buckle our seat belts and get ready to climb the mountain. We look out and sometimes we can see the drop, other times we cannot. As the ride continues, fear and worry may set in but there is a realization, we will somehow reach the top.

At the top, we can see everything which surrounds us. Once we get a clear view and enjoy seeing the sky and admiring the surroundings, you drop. Down the hill we go. It seems life begins to fall apart when we are in the valley. Then, we go up another hill. Most of the times these smaller hills may turn into a big hill, but there is still a journey and lessons to learn. This cycle continues until we are safely back at the Boarding Station. We get off this ride, and then go to wait for another ride. Just like the hills and valleys in our lives, we go up, and we go down just to ride the rollercoaster all over again. Maybe this is a big one, maybe it's smaller. The point is sometimes we know, sometimes we don't know how the journey in life will turn out. What I do know is every decision we make, whether consciously or subconsciously, affects the way we live and see life. This is where we get to make decisions.

Each time you ride the rollercoaster you can discover nuggets along the way. You learn about what twists and turns you don't like and the ones you do like. The path forward is not a straight line. You move forward but may need to circle back. You need to be aware of what seat you are in. Stop fighting and learn from the dips. The next time you're faced with something familiar, you will face this situation, and the bottom of the hill will not be so bad. Appreciate the time to learn. Don't rush as there are nutrients you need to grow.

Understanding who I am, has been a constant struggle. I always defined myself by material things, how I looked compared to others and what I thought I needed to do in order to 'fit' in and 'please' others. Every instance of this kind of thinking led me into darkness.

There are certain things in life you have to know:

- Who are you?
- What are your goals and what's the plan to get there?
- What is your purpose?
- What resources do you have and what resources do you need?
- Who will benefit from what you know?

Vulnerability requires compassion to yourself and empathy toward others. If you're striving to live a perfect life, you'll miss out on living. As long as you rely on other people to make your life work, you will be a slave to the circumstances they live in. Don't let your ego get in the way of your progress. Be authentically you. Start seeing and treating yourself as the most important person in the world. This begins with being honest with yourself and others. In order to begin again, or reinvent yourself, you have to live in the present moment. Here are affirmations that reminds me to put myself first:

- **I live a fearless life.** I'm not afraid anymore. Experience has thickened my skin in a world where it's easy to live in fear. You have to remember you have the ability to think, create and make the decisions that work for you ... not for others. In the end, you have to get to a point where you cannot worry about what someone thinks or says about you when you are living your truth.
- **Love is my main intent.** When I love myself, I am free to love others.
- **I forgive myself for any fear or insecurity.** I will no longer fear failure and rejection.
- **I'm a quiet storm who will get things done.** Every resource I need will come to me effortlessly.
- **I'm validating myself from the inside out.** The way I appear on the outside reflects who I am on the inside.
- **I will stop reliving or dwelling in the past.** I will focus on moving forward and only reminiscence on great things.
- **I will stop denying myself happiness.** I will live to be happy and enjoy being happy.
- **I will stop taking on too much 'stuff'.** I will know how much I can handle and understand when enough is enough. It is okay to say no.

- **I will stop doubting my abilities.** I will see my skills, talents, and gifts as they were given to me to use.
- **In my abundance, I will bless others.** My increase will be for me to be a blessing to others as I take care of myself first.
- **The essence of who I am, is beautiful, soft, and gentle.** My inner person is kind, gentle, and beautiful.
- **It's okay for me to connect with my inner child and to go on play dates and have fun.** My biggest attractions are finding ways to enjoy life. Going back to the sand box is what I enjoy doing.
- **I'm full of wisdom.** The wisdom that I have within is deep down on the inside of me and is evident in the decisions I make.
- **I can breathe.** I have learned how to inhale and exhale and not hold my breath, especially when I am under pressure.
- **Abundance flows easily and freely through me.** I am a well of plenty and more than enough.
- **I'm free.** There are no chains and shackles holding me from walking in newness.
- **I create my reality.** I have total control of my life to make it what I want it to be.
- **Serving others serves me.** The ability to help others gives me strength to handle my own affairs.
- **I play. I create. I succeed.** I take time to enjoy life, so I am free in my creativity expression which helps me to succeed in life.

- **Joy is my highest purpose.** I pull on the joy that is within because it is there no matter what happens.
- **I'm a powerful creator.** I was created to produce and make things happen.
- **I never lack.** Everything I need is within me.
- **I must live in the present.** I cannot move backwards; I have to live now.
- **Suspend Ego!** Live out the center and work from there. Get out of your own way.
- **I'm imperfect and I'm enough!** All of my imperfections are there to push me forward.
- **What's shareable is bearable.** When you share your story with someone, you are going through your healing process.
- **I can always begin again.** In life, I have learned to start over if it is necessary.
- **I'm worthy of being loved.** I have been designed to be loved by others and to love myself.
- **I'm powerful.** I am a force in the earth that causes greatness to happen.
- **I forgive myself.** Everything happened in divine order. There is space for me.
- **My heart is my safe space.** This is where I find out who I am.
- **I attract people who honor and respect the person I am.** I am a magnet that attracts greatness.
- **I'm strong.** I have the ability to stand.

- **I cannot rely on drugs or alcohol to suppress my feelings.** I refuse to depend on false gratification.
- **I will no longer settle for less than what I'm worth.** I realize that I am worth more than gold.
- **If somebody has to be happy, it's going to be me.** I will make sure that my day is filled with happiness.
- **I love and trust my imagination**. I enjoy the creative process.
- **I'm a thought leader.** My thoughts are ten steps ahead.
- **I'm classy.** I have style and charisma.
- **I'm a connector.** I connect others with purpose.
- **I advocate for the rights of all humans.** I stand for what is right for myself and others.
- **The world is waiting for my vision.** Every morning that I rise, my vision unfolds, and others stand in great anticipation for it to be revealed.

As you work on yourself, you will discover many people aren't on your level. When that happens, it's not you, it's the other person who cannot relate to you. Higher levels require higher thinking. When people see this, you will begin to see in between the circumstances you encounter. When you begin to glow, others want to stunt your growth (crabs in a bucket). When rejection happens, better is always on the other end. You just have to learn to control it so you can be the best you.

How do you love yourself?

_____
_____
_____
_____
_____
_____
_____
_____
_____
_____
_____

What do you need to do to begin loving yourself at the highest level possible?

_____
_____
_____
_____
_____
_____
_____
_____
_____
_____
_____

To be vulnerable is to be honorable. Take your ups and downs equally. The downs are what gets you to the ups.

~CONSUELO

SELF–LOVE

Today I'm grateful at working towards directing love to myself. I'm thankful I'm learning not to take anything personal, and I'm also learning to be more trustful and confident about the things I already have and also the things I desire. I'm becoming the ultimate person I want to be and deserve to be.

~VALERIE

Self-love is a term that took me a long time to understand. As a teenage mom and as a single mom, most of my time was dedicated to making sure I nurtured and cared for others. That often left me hanging in the rafters clinging tightly to sanity. Each of us has to learn what it is we can do to show love to ourselves. No one can love you better than you can love yourself. In a counseling session, I was asked to list the initials of five people that meant the most to me, and I listed them in order of importance. I listed them pretty fast because it was an easy list for me to create. I then shared my list with my

119

counselor and was asked, "What's your first initial?" I responded, "V". He then asked me where I was on the list. I wasn't there. I should have been at the top of the list. I thought about everyone else except myself.

Setbacks, disappointments, and fears across time leave us with a single question about Love. *Can I love again? Will I love again?* Those are the questions we ask ourselves over and over again. I gave up on finding love and realized much later that energy needed to be redirected to myself. Love does not begin with pleasing someone else. Love does not break your heart unless you allow it to. The type of love I am speaking of is internal. It's time for you to start loving yourself.

It was not until I became an empty nester and was forced to take a break from any serious relationship for me to realize I did not really know what I wanted. I was so busy pleasing others thinking it made them love me more, I forgot about myself. This can happen unintentionally but bring one an awakening.

After my last daughter left for College, I was happy. Rejoicing that both of my daughters were now enrolled in college. After a week or so later, I needed more food and went grocery shopping. I began shopping for the things I always buy. Since grocery shopping was routine, I did not think I was cooking for one. It took me 20 minutes to realize that I was shopping for my daughters and not for myself. I went back to the front of the store and put back everything and started over. I stood there with the shopping cart in the store, looked around and thought to myself, what do I like to eat? I had to stop and take inventory on what I liked.

In the book, *Sisters of the Yam* (Hooks, 2005), the author states, "Understanding love as a life-force ... enables us to see clearly, where love is, there can be no disenabling, disempowering, or life destroying abuse." With that quote in mind, I observed the following fact ... Love Heals!

*　　*　　*

You cannot live with love and pain at the same time. You cannot live with love and fear at the same time. You have to consciously choose one over the other. I commit to being my highest priority. There is nothing selfish about the statement. My growth is important. I had to learn how to focus on what I need and still need to learn about myself. I have to pay attention to my emotions, my thoughts, and my intentions. When I do this, I know things will flow to me effortlessly because I am living and leading with authenticity, and I Love myself.

- *Speak your truth. If we don't share it or write about it, we can't get passed it.*
- *Conversation before confrontation ... remember grace and love?*
- *It's not how you fall down; it's how you get up.*
- *Challenges are opportunities. Never stop fighting!*
- *A lie will only last until the truth arrives.*
- *Take responsibilities for your actions, decisions, and experiences ... own it!*
- *Be true to yourself.*

- *Call me fearless. On the other side of fear is euphoria.*

My happiness Matters.

It takes courage to be soul-full
~REVEREND JACQUELINE HAWKINS

We are not defined by life circumstances; our reaction is what matters. Two words, attitude and success are your superpowers.

* * *

My wish for you is respect, wisdom, and good judgment. I wish you the ability to think critically for yourself in your desire to help and support others. I wish you the ability to analyze and problem solve. I wish you would become surrounded by new ideas and your mind be activated to a higher level of being. I wish your desire for knowledge, truth, and understanding would come to fruition, and it aids you in enhancing your memory so you can learn to live in harmony and truth. I commit to helping you through this. You will never have to walk alone.

Are you living or are you existing?

_____

_____

_____

_____

_____

_____

KNOW COURAGE

Therapy can be the acceleration out of a stagnant pattern, the support needed for an important change, the guidance for rebuilding self-esteem.

~SARK

The Wizard of Oz was my favorite childhood Movie. I watched it almost every week. I know the entire script. There were times I pretended to be all the characters where I did the dance moves and dialogue. In the movie, Dorothy and her dog, Toto, were swept away as a tornado tossed her home into another dimension. When Dorothy awakened, she found herself in a land called Oz and learned her house landed on the Wicked Witch of the east and killed her. A group of munchkins were happy because they were finally free.

The Wicked Witch of the west appeared angry that her sister was killed. Her sister's ruby slippers were still on her feet. When the Wicked Witch of the East tried to remove the slippers from her sister's feet, the Wicked Witch of the east shriveled up and dissipated in thin air. The shoes appeared on Dorothy's feet at the blessing of Glinda the Good Witch. Glinda told Dorothy that the shoes must be powerful and to never take them off her feet.

The story of the Wizard of Oz symbolizes the full circle of my life experience; there were times I was swept away and lost my will because of my emotional state.

Home should be a place of peace where we are balanced, centered, and surrounded by the positive energy where we can create. Think about it this way: The Tornado, that swept Dorothy and her dog Toto away, symbolizes how quickly we can get involved in a situation and not know how to navigate it. We enter a dream state where we can create a negative or positive outcome. At first, everything may seem scary until a mentor (Glinda the Good Witch) and other supporters (munchkins) point us in the right direction and coaches us throughout the journey. Along the way, we are given tools (critical thinking friends) that will help us get back home. The lion who needed courage, the tinman who needed a heart, and the scarecrow who needed a brain were the critical thinking friends Dorothy met.

Here are reasons why we need to have our minds renewed, our hearts soften, and courage to be conquerors:

- A brain so we can think again.

- A heart so we can love again.

- Courage to help us find our way back to the right place.

Along the way, several obstacles keep us from getting home:

- The Wicked Witch of the East is the negativity that tries to block our success. They are jealous of what we have.

- We think we have reached the end, but another barrier is thrown in our way. This is Dorothy meeting the Wizard for the first time and being tasked with an activity that seems impossible.

- Encountering the negative energy again, we find ourselves navigating through the obstacle and accidentally find the way out. It was supposed to happen that way.

- Now possessing the tool that we need to get home; we return to a previous barrier and can now overcome it.

- We get to what we think is the end, and we realize that everything we needed, we already have.

- Oz represents the way home, a place that is already in our hearts. It was buried but now it's out.

- We find out that we already are at home because we affirmed it in our minds. The experience is a reminder that we have the power to change our situation. we had it from the beginning.

Courage is the ability to fight through fear. Courage is the strength to face the day even when we don't want to. Courage is the strength to say I need help. Courage is also the strength to stand up for what we know is right and fair. Don't be afraid to seek justice, don't be afraid to speak out. As I mentioned earlier, what's shareable is bearable and to live this requires courage and vulnerability.

Vulnerability requires compassion and empathy. Vulnerability is the courage needed to expose the issues we fight without being afraid of being harmed. I had to rise out of my comfort zone and allow myself to be vulnerable, so I could be better understood. Using 'rise' as an acronym, we have **resilience**. We have the **intelligence** to navigate difficulty. We are **strong** and strength reminds us to look at a difficult situation differently. Once we can view our situation with a critical eye, we become **enlightened** about what we experience and **evolve**.

<u>R</u>esilient

<u>I</u>ntelligent

<u>S</u>trong

<u>E</u>mpowered, enlightened, evolve

Remember who you are and **<u>RISE</u>**.

What have you been through that reminded you that you had everything you needed within you?

_____
_____
_____
_____
_____
_____
_____
_____
_____
_____
_____
_____
_____
_____
_____
_____
_____
_____
_____
_____

KNOW BOUNDARIES

I want to be happy. I want to experience true love. I want to know what it genuinely feels like to be loved and cared for by someone else. I think I'm afraid to love and I'm afraid of love. To think of myself in a healthy relationship is scary because I don't know what it looks like. Just about every relationship I've had with a male was based on lust. Almost all of those relationships ended in disaster. I don't want that anymore. I can't take that anymore. Now the question is, what do I need to do to not get that anymore?

~VALERIE

What are your non-negotiables? What self-values have you intertwined with your non-negotiables. What experiences have you had that makes something non-negotiable? You cannot have non-negotiables if you don't set boundaries.

Boundaries have always been a struggle for me. I buried myself behind the mask of wanting people to like me often at my own expense. In relationships, I always did what made my partner happy. If my partner was happy, I was happy. If my partner was sad, I was sad. I took sadness one step further to try to remedy the situation so we both could be happy again. Now, I know that is called **co-dependency**.

Co-dependency is an emotional and psychological connection to someone and something. There were times I pleased people because it felt good but wasn't good at all. There were times where I felt like I could not function or focus without using marijuana and alcohol. I fed on the needs of others instead of feeding myself.

Not knowing boundaries led me to Emotions Anonymous at the advice of my therapist. Just like Alcohol Anonymous (AA), Emotion's Anonymous (EA) challenges those things which make you co-dependent. One of the most fascinating things I experienced in EA is that what I was facing wasn't really bad. I did not compare my situations to others, but it was good to be safe enough to be able to talk out my feelings to others.

At my first EA meeting, I just observed. I did not want to speak much because I did not know what to expect. What I appreciated most was hearing how others coped with their reality. EA is about becoming emotionally heathy, which is a key to mental health. I did not realize there was a 12-step program to help you through. Although, the twelve steps of Emotions Anonymous are the same 12 steps in Alcoholics Anonymous, the steps are applied in a different manner.

Step 1: We admitted we were powerless over our emotions – our lives have become unmanageable.

Step 2: We have come to believe a power greater than ourselves could restore us to sanity.

Step 3: We have to decide to turn our will and our lives over to the care of God ... as we understand Him.

Step 4: We have made a searching and fearless moral inventory of ourselves.

Step 5: We have admitted to God, to ourselves, and to another human being the exact nature of our wrongs.

Step 6: We are entirely ready to have God remove all of these defects of character.

Step 7: We have humbly asked God to remove our shortcomings.

Step 8: We have made a list of all the persons we harmed and became willing to make amends with them all.

Step 9: We made direct amends to such people wherever possible, except when to do so would injure them or others.

Step 10: We continued to take personal inventory and when we were wrong, promptly admitted it.

Step 11: We sought through prayer and meditation to improve our conscious contact with God as we understood Him, praying only for knowledge of His will for us and the power to carry it out.

Step 12: We have had a spiritual awakening as the result of steps, we tried to carry this message and to practice these principles in our affairs.

(www.emotionsanonymous.com)

For us to heal from co-dependency, we must create boundaries which is one of the things I continue to work on. It's easy to let someone into my life, yet difficult to remove them from my life. Dignity is non-negotiable. You are worthy of honor and respect.

If you are not working on your goals and dreams,
you are working on an excuse.

~VERNITA KING

The critical link to move toward healthy emotions is you. Setting boundaries is another decision you can make to take one step toward emotional healing. The steps are not easy to get through. You have to take it one step at a time, as I did. You also have to be compassionate with yourself and realize it's okay to have more time to work on a single step. They are not meant to be completed in one day anyway. This requires a mindset change. You have to want to get out of the rabbit hole and acknowledge you need help.

Fifteen years later, I still struggle with relationships because I am working on creating boundaries. Knowing I need to start creating boundaries is one step in the right direction. Having someone available to hold me accountable is the second step. Loving myself just the way I am is the most important step. Here are my non-negotiables. This is the way it has to be if I am taking care of me.

- No longer will I hang around liars. If you lie to me, I'm out. This includes omitting information. I want the whole story the first time.

- No longer will I purposely overwhelm myself to say yes to something when I really mean no.

- I decide what I want to do with my time. Time is valuable, and I will use it to do things I want to do.

- If I don't know in advance, there's a strong possibility you won't get a favorable response.

- No longer will I settle for one way communication in a relationship.

- I cannot own someone else's problem. I can be compassionate and empathetic but when it's a 'you' problem, that's your problem.

- I will no longer doubt my intuition.

- I will only have expectations if you give me a reason to.

As you are creating boundaries, be careful what you share and who you share it with. Everybody who looks like they're on your team is not. This is a hard truth, and it must be repeated regularly. I have had plenty of experiences where people pretended to be in my corner, pretended to be supportive, pretended they cared, pretended to be helpful. At the end of all of the pretending, I was the one left feeling like a dagger went through the spine of my back and exited through the center of my heart. It hurts to think that those you trust may be behind your back wishing you ill will. Know the people who are really on your team and don't be surprised if the list becomes extremely short.

What boundaries have you set?

_____

_____

_____

_____

_____

_____

_____

_____

How do you feel after you comply to the decision you made?

_____

_____

_____

_____

_____

_____

_____

_____

FORGIVENESS

Forgiveness represents the path forward. Forgiveness leads you away from the results of the past and towards making the changes that are needed. Forgiveness can take the guilt away. The first person I had to forgive was myself. Forgiveness is for you.

Self-forgiveness is the most powerful gift you can give yourself. What we must recognize is sometimes it takes pain to change the trajectory of your life. Death, whether physical or supernatural, can be the greatest teacher. Think about it this way ... you are an individual called 'me'. You cannot control the actions of others, but what you can control is how you respond. Responding in the heat of the moment is never the correct answer.

There are things that drive me 'numb'. I use the word numb because it always stops me and leaves me feeling stuck. These are things which continually encouraged me to overeat, to overspend, and to not care about myself. Here are some of the things that drove me 'numb':

- Broken promises
- Constant negativity
- Lack of support
- Rejection
- Feeling powerless
- Fear
- Loneliness
- Lack of control
- Being misunderstood

When something or someone hurts us, the best thing we can do is take a step back, cool down, and remove ourselves from the negative energy which tends to overtake us when something goes wrong. We also must do an ego check.

I had to ask myself these questions, "What is it keeping me stuck feeling like I cannot move forward? What chains are holding me down that I need to break?" I must stop trying to build a new building on an old foundation. I must stop being hard on myself and know I possess the power within myself to turn things around. Stop putting myself down. Stop trying to fit into situations I don't fit into. How can I lift others when I keep myself down? These are statements and questions I must say and ask myself repeatedly. There were several different parts of me I was pulling and waving for help on the inside. Help always comes once you forgive and release. Forgiveness is for you not the other person. You keep yourself in bondage. You hold yourself in a pattern of repeating the same thing never to be released then you start pointing the finger at everyone saying it is not your fault.

I have held many grudges. By holding these grudges, I held myself back from the blessings that were waiting on me which I could not see because I was blinded by loss, grief, and many other negative feelings I allowed to hold me back.

It's easy to hold a grudge. It's easy to become paralyzed and wrapped in the victim mentality; however, that route is destructive, unproductive, and depressing. It shows your lack of accountability and your unwillingness to take responsibility for yourself. Own your 'stuff'.

Forgiveness is the ticket I used to remove the 'devil on my back' an old saying from individuals who have experienced sleep paralysis. I suffered from sleep paralysis for years. Imagine waking up in your sleep, consciously aware of being awake yet you're paralyzed in your own body. You cannot move. You cannot speak and oftentimes, I thought I was dead or dying. This is how much I allowed the spirit of unforgiveness to literally weigh me down.

The ticket out of this phase of my life was to begin to forgive those I felt wronged me or hurt me in anyway. I needed to be free. I needed to restore my energy.

I make phone calls to take my energy back and settle misunderstandings. This is not an easy task. It will take courage and it will take strength. You will have to remove your ego and approach the situation with humility. This is how you can walk away and keep your dignity.

I have had my share of conversations where people did not feel like they wronged me, or they refused to accept the responsibility of what I perceived was a wrongdoing. This is when I again have to remind myself forgiveness is for me. Forgiveness is the route to my freedom and the necessary relief from the bondage my mental state would put me in.

When you operate from unforgiveness, you also operate from a state of fear and fear allows your mind to create stories and scenarios in your mind which don't exist. Then you go down the rabbit hole of negative self-doubt, negative self-talk, regret and what I'd call a rough and tough attitude which creates a wall no one can penetrate.

* * *

Letter from Ex-Husband

Dear Val,

You are an amazing, beautiful, and smart young lady. You have achieved things no one thought was possible. You were determined and you survived. Now one of the biggest tasks in front of you is to acknowledge and to become more aware of your value. You are extremely precious and should only spend your time, thoughts, and energy on those things and people which serve you and make you feel good.

~REGINALD SIMMONS

When I got divorced in 2014, it was my fault. I cheated, and I own that. My ex-husband would have given me the world if he could. Now I can reflect on my mistake, I have learned I was more in love with the idea of being married rather than actually being married and creating a partnership. I was independent. I was strong willed and controlled the relationship. I treated him as if I had to take care of him and thought I could hold my own. I was unaware of the hurt I was causing my ex-husband while we were married.

I traveled a lot for work and left him at home with my daughters. I did not know how to be present in his life. I still did not know what love looked like even though I thought I did. When you talk about someone having a cold heart, you are talking about me. I left my ex-husband out in the cold on one of the coldest days of the year. I left him with no money.

My ex-husband and I separated for a few; we even went to counseling. Divorce was inevitable. I gave up on trying to make things work. I did not speak to my ex-husband for several years until I got this email:

Greetings Val,

I hope all is well and this message finds you in lifted spirit and harmony. For some reason or the other, you have crossed my mind on a few occasions the past couple of weeks. I hope you know all is well in the universe and always will be well.

Lately, I have been reading a lot of Danielle Laporte writings. For some reason she really talks to my spirit.

Through her writings, meditation and the power of the mantra 'see yourself in others' I have been able to connect and engage with the universe in amazing ways. Anyhow below is something I discovered a while back. During my last couple of meditations, I was told to teach you what I learned. I know it sounds crazy, but here we go. This came to me in meditation, and I pass it to you in love.

The reason why we have a hard time healing past pain and trauma is because the past is still happening, not just in the continuum of time but in the subconscious these events are still alive and well. It's a form of energy ... difficult to explain, but just follow me on this. Here is what you need to do. First look in a mirror and say the statements. Say them 'til you have it somewhat memorized. Maybe do it every morning or before you go to bed.

> *I give myself permission to:*
> - *Have feelings,*
> - *Make mistakes,*
> - *Be honest,*
> - *Not have all the answers,*
> - *Take care of me first,*
> - *Not care what other people think,*
> - *Say no,*
> - *Enjoy the moment,*
> - *Be direct,*
> - *Have fun, and*
> - *Be happy.*

When you feel you have it memorized, then you're ready for Step 2. This is the most challenging part. Meditate and quiet your mind as much as possible. Now go back to 19-year-old Valerie. Go to that time and try to recall the house or apartment, the room, etc. You are to grab the younger version of yourself and put her in front of a mirror, give the both of you a big warm hug, have her look directly and repeat the phrases you memorized from earlier.

After I read the email, I contemplated on whether I should respond or not. I felt a release but yet, the situation was not complete, and I still had some emptiness. What I needed to do was become accountable for what I had done by apologizing to my ex-husband and I did. The conversation resulted in being extremely pleasant. However, he used this opportunity to express his sadness and disappointment. I knew this was a time in which I needed to listen. It was not the time to get defensive and try to justify why things happened the way they did. I listened and took full responsibility. To this day, my ex-husband and I have a cordial relationship, something I did not think was possible. I now know the impossible is possible. I forgave myself as well and never had to relive or focus on the divorce ever again.

*   *   *

In 2015, I found out I was pregnant. After telling everyone I was an empty nester by the age of 40, here I was in a situation I thought could not happen or would never happen. I called the baby's father to tell him I was pregnant. He hung up on me which was something that took me by surprise. I immediately called him right back and he answered. In a nutshell, he told me to have an abortion and he would have nothing to do with my pregnancy. I considered abortion thinking this could be the karma I created when I got divorced. I was devastated. Shortly after the pregnancy, I started a journal specifically to write regarding the pregnancy to the baby.

Here is the first entry- August 10, 2015:

I found out I was pregnant on July 31. I knew something wasn't right. I missed my cycle and had an overwhelming feeling of being pregnant. While thinking I could no longer get pregnant after a difficult pregnancy and labor with my younger daughter, I continued to be in denial since April of 1999. Here I'm, pregnant with you on the inside.

I saw you yesterday (well at least your temporary home) via ultrasound. It became real at that moment. You are growing in my belly. My blood pressure is running a bit high, so I have to relax. I want you to come out healthy and strong. I know you will. Feeling alone in this journey, I began to create a village of supporters. People I love and trust mutually. Know that you are already loved. I'm not sure how often I'll write but know I'm thinking about you. I love you and I can't wait to meet you.

Journal Entry - August 26, 2015:

I heard your heartbeat for the first time – 150 beats per minute. You are real and you are living inside of me. I'm watching you grow and develop right in front of my eyes. My prayer is for a healthy pregnancy and a healthy baby. I know all will be well ... especially when the Diclegis kicks in. This morning sickness is lasting all day and is kicking my butt.

Random Journal Entry:

Your heartbeat is going strong at 174 beats per minute. They got the measurement so quick I didn't even know they got it. In a couple of weeks, I'll know your gender. I can't wait to find out your sex and have another ultrasound. No worries here. All will be well!

I struggled through this pregnancy alone. My pregnancy was already high risk because of my age, and several other high risk factors including obesity and high blood pressure. I was sent to a maternal-fetal medicine specialist who would take over my care. Ultrasounds every two weeks and every test imaginable because I don't know the health history of my birth parents.

Journal Entry - October 4, 2015:

For the last several days, I have been working on surrendering. I had an ultrasound a couple of days ago and the doctor became disturbed and concerned with your brain and your face. In this ultrasound picture you are waving to me. Surely there can't be anything wrong. Of course, when I look at the picture, you look fine. In the end, the prognosis may not be good, but I know God gave you to me for more reasons than I can ever imagine. You're doing a lot of moving around and dancing and rolling in the ultrasound. Please know none of this is because of you and if possible, I will always hope and encourage you.

Thirteen weeks into the pregnancy, the doctor noticed the ultrasound pictures were a bit abnormal. The nasal bone was flat and this I learned could mean there was a genetic issue with the pregnancy. Doctors requested I undergo genetic testing. The same day, I had my blood drawn and called to inform the father. He was not interested in hearing what I had to say. About a week or so later, I received the test results. All clear on my end. I even learned I was having a boy. I was excited about having a son; however, I was not excited about having to raise another child alone and on my own as this was becoming my reality.

Things went downhill pretty quickly from there. I never expected this chain of events to become a part of my destiny.

Journal Entry - October 23, 2015:

This past Wednesday was my appointment and the ultrasound to see how you are doing. Unfortunately, I got the devastating news that you have Alobar holoprosencephaly (HPE) which means your brain didn't fully develop. You also have some facial abnormalities because of the lack of brain development. All I can say is it's not your fault neither is it mine. This condition is 100% incompatible with life. Only 3% of babies with this condition make it to full term. Shortly after labor and delivery you would die. I had some choices to make. I could carry you until you decided to let go, or I could terminate the pregnancy. I made the devasting decision to terminate the pregnancy. I don't want you to suffer any longer. The procedure will take place tomorrow. I have to fly to Orlando to have the abortion because the laws in Texas for people like me suck! I decided to name you Ethan Enoch Peterson. Ethan means strong. You are extraordinarily strong; you are a fighter. Especially because you decided to stay and try to overcome this. I chose Enoch because in the bible, God snatched Enoch from the earth to walk with God. In essence, he disappeared to go to a better place. I know God is snatching you away and you will be walking with God, by my side. I'm blessed you were able to come into my life. You have taught me unbelievably valuable lessons, many of which will be with me for the rest of my life. You were here for a reason, and you fulfilled your purpose. Now I'm giving you back to God. Believe me, chilling with God is much better than chilling down here on earth. Please know I will always love you and carry you forever in my heart. It's definitely not goodbye, it's see ya later.

At the time of my pregnancy, there was a law in Texas called House Bill 2 (HB2). HB2 required abortion clinics to have hospital-like standards. This included specific measurements on doors, new anesthesia requirements, and doctors have admitting privileges at a hospital no less than 30 miles away. This was added to the mandatory ultrasound and counseling, and a 24-hour wait period. There was a large amount of abortion clinics shut down as they did not meet the requirements the state issued this new law without any funding.

When it was time for me to terminate the pregnancy, I did not know about HB2. After my doctor told me what my options were and I made my decision, I asked the doctor how we would proceed with the procedure. It was then when he referred me to planned parenthood. I was confused as to why my doctor who knew my case and whom I trusted could not perform the abortion. He informed me because of the laws, many clinics had to shut down and there would be a three-four week waiting period. At 20 weeks, abortion is banned in Texas. The fact there was a waiting list not only angered me, but it left me confused as to why my body was being legislated.

I told my doctor I could not wait long. My mental health and my emotional health had reached the bottom of the barrel. I was suffering. Seeing the anguish on my face, he made a call and was able to get me an appointment two weeks away. At first, I accepted but when the clinic called, I realized I could not. When I spoke to the nurse at the clinic in Texas, she informed me of the procedure. She also said I would need to make four separate appointments: Day one: an ultrasound and counseling. I was also told I should prepare to be in the clinic all day. After the ultrasound and counseling, Day two: would be a 24-hour waiting period. Day three: the procedure would begin, and Day four: I would have to come back the next day to begin the procedure. As anger and emotional distress continued to cloud my mind, I told the nurse I would not be able to schedule the appointment. Not knowing what to do, I immediately called my aunt and my friend and shared with them my dilemma. It was then I noticed I had to leave the state of Texas to get an abortion.

Still not understanding this and feeling like I was living outside of my body; my friend knew of a Hospital in Florida. I immediately located the number and called the clinic immediately. When I called to my surprise, the doctor answered the phone. I explained my situation to him and amazingly he told me he could get the procedure done in one day and could schedule me for the appointment the next day.

Feeling a sense of relief, I scheduled the appointment and gave myself a day to fly to Florida to get the procedure done. After scheduling the appointment, I purchased a last-minute ticket to Orlando, rented a car, got a hotel room, and had the money for the procedure as I found out this was an elective and not covered by insurance. Till this day I have a hard time understanding why this was an elective procedure. My son did not have a brain. I could not control this.

I was blessed to have a friend meet me in Florida and walk with me through the procedure. Emotionally distraught, having someone there that is a friend made me feel better. I was already uneasy about going through with the abortion and having to go to another state to have this process done.

The doctors and the nurses were compassionate and gave me a high level of quality care. I had my own nurse, my own waiting room which looked like a living room and time to process what was getting ready to happen. Within me, I touched my stomach and spoke to Ethan, the nurse held my hand and just like that, the procedure was over.

Journal Entry - November 8, 2015:

I told your dad about your death via text. I couldn't hold it in any longer. It was bothering me so much. I'm aware he didn't deserve to know but I was also aware I needed to bring closure to the situation.

At this moment, I realized I had to forgive myself first and then I would be in a better position to forgive him.

While still wounded and heartbroken, I gained enough courage to forgive and to cut the cord. I vomited that night. I sat in the bathtub and cried like a baby. I released the frustration and the anger. I cleansed myself of the negative energy I was holding in my body. I then got out of the bathroom, washed my face, and went to bed. I was determined to awake to a brand-new day in which I could start all over and begin again. Ethan is the strength that has my back.

KNOW YOUR VOICE

Almost three years later ... here you are again showing me what my purpose is. Days from your due date I'm here in Washington D.C Sharing our story with the nation. I'm sharing my story because I matter, and I continue to get stronger as I share my story with those who are against abortion rights. People will disagree with me but that's alright. They wouldn't dare volunteer to walk in my shoes.

~VALERIE

Stand up for what is right and fair. Seek justice for yourself and seek justice for others. Hold yourself and others accountable. Stop being angry, do something. It's time to shift our thinking. Fear can break you down, but love provides liberation, and instills a sense of confidence. I learned how to fight for humanity and fight for myself, but the fight for myself came first. I can no longer hide when I see someone being harmed. When you are your truth, confidence fills your soul and your passion for humanity and human rights shine bright.

After the abortion, I looked for ways to minimize the hurt I encountered from the experience. I found a group which supports women who had late abortions due to fetal anomalies. I listened to them share their stories and they listened to mine. After sharing, I was asked if I wanted to share the story with a woman who was advocating for reproductive healthcare in Texas. At the time, she was the Executive Director of a non-profit organization. Not knowing the ridiculous law, HB2 in Texas, she was headed for the supreme court of the United States, she asked if I was interested in sharing my story. I did not have to think about it. I knew my voice needed to be heard. Just like the decision I made to terminate the pregnancy I knew it needed to be done.

Being an abortion advocate can create volatile situations. Many people in this fight face harassment and some killed. I was asked if I wanted to be anonymous and I declined. The experience was mine, and I wanted people to know I am a human being with a real experience. I was speaking my truth and my hurt. In the abortion fight, you can also be dehumanized and shamed. I did not and don't care about what people think about me. I don't own their feelings; I only own mine.

I was asked to share my experience at an abortion rally on the steps of the Supreme Court while the HB2 case arguments were being made. I had the support of my Mother and my Mentor who stood right beside me while I was speaking. When I first started speaking, I was nervous. I was interrupted by a pro-lifer who yelled and screamed I was fake which made me angry, and the nervousness immediately passed. I continued to share.

After I spoke, there were several women who admired my courage. They shared their abortion stories with me but to family and friends, they used miscarriage to shield themselves from the judgment an abortion can bring.

My advocacy did not stop at the Supreme Court, it continues. I have shared my story in newspapers, magazines, by way of documentaries, through plays and in state appellate courts and with local and federal legislators. I don't share to get sympathy. I share because it boggles my mind how my decision and my body can be legislated and treated as if it belongs to the government. Frankly, it is nobody's business. Because we live at a time where that is no longer the case, we have to continue to fight for the ability to obtain reproductive healthcare with confidentiality, no shame, and no barriers.

Today is the day that I had rested enough to realize how precious I am and how valuable I am. This week I was given a large platform that enabled me to come out of my shell. For the first time in a long time, I felt like I belonged. I was able to say the word abortion, defend myself and not be afraid to do so. It made me realize that I am a force to be reckoned with and a lot of people have been missing out on the authentic me. I am love; I show love.

~VALERIE

What fight for rights are you drawn to?

_____
_____
_____
_____
_____
_____
_____
_____
_____
_____
_____
_____
_____

How can you use your story to advocate for others?

_____
_____
_____
_____
_____
_____
_____
_____
_____
_____
_____
_____
_____

Take your ups and downs equally. The downs are what gets you through the ups.

~CONSUELO

NO REGRETS

The fact is you already know how to find yourself; you have just gotten distracted and disoriented. Once refocused, you will realize that you not only have the ability to find yourself, you have the ability to free yourself.

~MICHAEL SINGER

One question always gets asked of me is whether there is anything I would change in my journey. My response is, "No." Every experience I have shared with you, helped create the person I am today. Experience has taught me how to be grateful, how to be humble, and how to be a Servant Leader. Throughout my pain, I learned the true meaning of restoration, renewal, refocus, and relief. I had to reframe my thought process of what I have been through. I had to shift from a victim mentality to one of survival and growth. So, the journey continues. Not from a place of despair but from a place of love with a renewed sense of confidence, purpose, and meaning.

The most valuable commodity you can have is information. Information obtained by your own and other lived experiences, information obtained in a book, on TV, or through any other communication medium.

Any day can be your last day. What do you currently regret in your life, and how can you fix it to restore your sense of self?

EMOTIONAL REHABILITATION: COMPASSION AND SELF-CARE

Therapy has been a great part of self-care for me. I have been in therapy for over 22 years and have had several therapists. You have to be opened to sharing the deepest parts of your life with someone who cares for you and someone that can give you tools to keep moving forward in healthier ways. Some therapists are a right fit while others may not be suited for you. You must know when to separate yourself from a therapist that is not a right fit.

One of the things I appreciate learning in therapy, is the ability to implement the tools I received. These tools are supportive tools which can assist me in achieving harmony and balance. It has been said there are four primary portals in our body: The eye gate, the nose gate, the ear gate, and the mouth gate. As you can see, each gate represents an opening into your body (eyes, nose, ears, and mouth). Each of these gates are critical in achieving harmony and balance in your mind.

I. **Eye-Gate**: We have to be mindful of the things we allow ourselves to see. We also must remember, we have the ability to see things from a different perspective. We have to be aware of the things we watch on television, the things we choose to allow on our social media timelines, ever. It's been said the eyes are connected to your soul.

- **Dreams:** Dreams that I can remember go into my aforementioned dream journal that I review to make connections. It's important for me to write what I saw. I may be dreaming about a situation and how I should respond or dreaming about a person who died and is now in the role of guiding me and providing me messages.

- **Visualization:** I visualize those things I want to see manifest. In retrospect, I still struggle with changing the vision to what I desire.

Colors help with setting the atmosphere. Using colors to balance my mood came from one of my therapist:

- o White is pure and the manifestation of transformation.
- o Red and orange is for creativity.
- o Red represents love for self and love for others.
- o Yellow represents the sun which is energy that can give us the will power to move forward.
- o Green is the ability to look at something new to grow into and is also solution oriented.
- o Blue is related to the ocean. It is serenity and communication with God.
- o Purple is hope and faith and knowing that you can create anything out of loss.
- o Brown helps you to plant your feet that holds foundational principles intact.
- o Black is the combination of all the colors, and it is solid.

Mountains: They are still, will not move, and will always live in the present. The ability to look at a physical mountain and admiring its presence as a statement of I am secured!

Oceans: Looking at the ocean and realizing there are endless opportunities available. The waves representing a calming flow.

Sky: Looking at the sky reminds me there is a greater power than ourselves. Moon baths and sun baths are relaxing. The moon baths help to discover wonderment of the constellations of stars. The sun baths provide health benefits such as vitamin D and other nutrients our body needs.

- **Vision Boards**: 3D journaling which is using artifacts and pictures to manifest your desires.

- **Journaling:** Dream journal, gratitude journal, traveling journal, and daily emotional journal, or one journal for everything: Writing about how I'm seeing the world and reviewing my journal to see how far I have come and to see the things I still need to work on. It gives you relief to purge what is heavy on your heart. Keep your journal in a secret place under lock and key or in a safe.

II. **Nose Gate:** Things we smell and do with our nose can influence us also. What is it I'm smelling? Is it burnt or is it aromatic? Does it make me feel good or nauseous?

- **Aromatherapy:** I love the scent of lavender and use lavender as an essential oil in a diffuser as incense as well as scented candles. I like to keep the scent of lavender constant which is why a large portion of my body wash, lotion and oils are lavender. Lavender is a soothing scent which calms me down and relaxes me. It also supports my ability to sleep.

Your pulse points are where you can apply nice scents to calm you and relax you and give you energy. Apply your favorite scent to your wrist and neck, along with other parts on the body.

- **Breathing exercises:** Breathing is essential to life. Taking deep breaths pull in oxygen and exhaling air releases carbon dioxide. This is a tool I use when I find myself tensing up. I also use it to calm me during a time when I am stressed. I use it throughout the day when I am overwhelmed. For example, anxiety causes rapid heartbeats and taking deep breaths can reset my breathing rhythms.

III. **Ear Gate**: The things we hear and listen to:

- **Introspection:** Sitting in silence so I can receive messages on things I need to know.

- **Listening:** Listening is a deeper level of hearing. Hearing the perspective of a non-biased person who won't judge you and abuse the information you share.

This is something I am still working on becoming a better listener.

- **Music:** Positive melodies with positive lyrics and positive beats: smooth Jazz, instrumentals, nature sounds, and sound baths (frequencies and tones). Music has an effect on us. The rhythm and/or lyrics goes into our subconscious mind and brings back **positive** or negative thoughts. Positive lyrics can shift the entire room to change for the better. Operative word here is POSITIVE!

- **Silence:** The ability to be quiet enough to hear and catch negative thoughts running through your mind and change them to positive thoughts.

- **Affirmations:** Using your voice to hear your thoughts so you can see what you said. For example, repeating a phrase such as I love myself which allows it to get into your subconscious. In the movie the HELP one of the main affirmations is: *You is kind, you is smart, you is important.* Jesse Jackson would always say, "I AM SOMEBODY!" Speak it, know it, believe that it can manifest, and it is so!!!

IV. **Mouth Gate:** The mouth is a gate that can effectively take in and put out.

What we are putting in:
The things we eat and drink:

- It is essential for us to eat foods that give us the nutrition that we need to maintain a healthy diet. Certain foods cause illnesses for some and overeating too. Learn what your body can and cannot digest properly. Acknowledging food allergies is essential to your life.

  For many years, I carried 264 pounds on my 5'4" frame. Medically, I was considered morbidly obese. Upon reflection when I look at myself at that weight, I realized how much toxic weight I carried because I used food as a coping mechanism. Now, my weight is more in accordance with the BMI chart which increases my self-confidence.

- Drinking alcohol excessively can destroy our liver and kidneys. Our bodies require water, and we should drink a certain number of liters of water a day. Water flushes out our system, aids in circulation, and hydrates us. Be mindful of the nutritional value in certain drinks. Most diet drinks contain lots of glucose which is sugar.

- Smoking damages the lungs and releases bad odors from our pores and breath.

What is going out:
Listen to the words that we are saying because what we say becomes our reality. Also, what we say can cause harm to others. Be mindful of the tone of our words.

These are self-care techniques that does not cost us anything:

- **Unclench your jaw**. You'd be surprised at the amount of tension you're holding on your face unaware.

- **Breathe.** Take a deep breathe from your nose. Hold for seven seconds, slowly release it then start over again. This will help lower your heart rate and give you a reset.

- **Exercise.** I love walking my dog. This is an activity that not only brings me peace but allows me the opportunity to bond with my dog.

- **Emotional Intelligence.** Being able to be compassionate to others including myself. Knowing how to use empathy and compassion to adjust the way I react.

- **Being in nature.** I love walking on grass with my bare feet which makes me feel like one with the universe. I also hug trees to remind me I'm one with nature. Listening to birds chirping, the sound of a thunderstorms, rain, wind, and the sound of ocean waves.

- **Admiring water** reminds me to cleanse my body. I take showers in the morning and baths at night. Sometimes I take a bath or a shower in the middle of the day. Its relaxing and I hope its enjoyable for you.

- **Massage** as a way to detox from the inside out and enjoy the feeling of relaxation.

- **Sleep**, which is my favorite. Reminding myself it's okay to recharge at any time. Resting your body is important.

- **Naps** when I'm feeling a little sluggish and need to rest my brain, I take ten-to-fifteen-minute naps. It recharges my body.

- **The ability to listen to my body and do absolutely nothing for a day or two.** Most of the times I plan it, sometimes I don't. I call this a hard reset. Just don't get stuck there.

- **Cleaning.** I turn on some music and I clean the entire house. It may take me a day or two, but I have found it relaxing. Be aware of the music that you listen to if you choose this. Be sure to include upbeat music that empowers you. Not only will your home be beautiful, but it's also easier to sleep in a clean house and your overall mood should shift. This is also a good time to reflect and to listen. A lot of ideas have come to me while I was cleaning.

The last part of my Emotional Rehabilitation was to get an emotional support animal as I mentioned earlier. I chose a dog. A Pomeranian Husky Mix named Logan. I have had him since he was a puppy.

Logan was already given a name after he was born. Not only was he a pretty puppy, but he also carried the last name of my Grandmother. I knew when I got Logan that it would be fulfilling helping him mature. Logan was trained when I got him, so I did not spend too much time training him. While Logan is a super intelligent dog, he's also stubborn. Probably because I spoil him. Logan is my best friend and confidant. He can feel my energy and respond to how I feel. He listens to my rants and sympathizes with me. He comforts me on the days that I don't feel like doing anything. We are attached.

What would you put in your emotional care kit?

_____

_____

_____

_____

_____

_____

_____

_____

_____

_____

He Uses Human Instruments

~CHARLES E. GARRISON

There are many things in Life
we don't know.
Most of which we need in Life
to help us as we grow.
Our Father has set up a Special Plan
to show us where to go.
But He alone knows the way
so, it's up to Him to show.
He leads us to a person
who has somehow found the way.
A person who has seen the light
who'll help brighten up our day.
He Uses Human Instruments
for they know what to say.
For they have learned to trust in Him
and in their life, He'll stay.
Life is full of mysteries that keeps us far behind
But if we learn of Jesus,
He'll surely free our minds.
God uses Human Instruments
to help us all to find

that if we put our faith in Him,

He will give us life divine.

With God's blessings through me, His instrument.

DECISION-MAKING AND CHANGE

The first 90 days of 2018, my year of manifestation has brought about change. The most significant change is a change in my awareness. There has also been a change in what I allow myself to tolerate. In this season, I was forced to remove people out of my life and to replace them with people who care and support me.

~VALERIE

The only constant thing in life is change. It's a fact that many changes are challenging. The ability to change is sometimes wrapped in confusion. While the confusion and challenge of change remains, it is also true that change can inevitably make you better and help you reach the next level every time; only if you approach change in that state of mind. If you don't have a positive outlook on change you will constantly wonder, "Did I make the right choice or did I not?"

I learned I must become responsible and accountable for the decisions I make. Rather the decisions I make are good or bad, they create my reality. Things happen in our life that may feel forced on us and that we did not have a choice but what happens next is, we recognize our ability to make different choices that defies circumstance which has the power to change the outcome of a situation. Too often we allow our egos to drive decision-making which gets us nowhere.

Every day we subconsciously make decisions. We decide when we want to get up, we decide if we want to press the snooze button, we decide if we want to take a shower, or if we want to take a bath. Research shows, we make at least 10,000 decisions a day. Those 10,000 decisions turn into millions and millions of decisions over a lifetime. Because we get wrapped up in patterns and cycles, we often miss the opportunity to make better decisions.

To make the best decisions, we must think independently. Critical thinking allows us to ask ourselves questions and to reflect on information that needs to be synthesized and analyzed. We have to be careful because sometimes we can overthink. Our focus may be on what decision to make that we never make the decision which needs to be made. Not being able to decide brings a lot of anxiety and stress which is often accompanied by depression. Positive thinking will create positive results. If you get frustrated in your thinking, it's often because you cannot decide or you're overthinking. If we fail to decide, we are making an excuse not to change for the better.

Making decisions for the growing list of concerns is hard. Realizing that you need to consider changes that may need to occur is even harder. Decision-making and change go hand in hand. This can be scary. You know you need to change, but you don't want to change because you are comfortable where you are. You may be afraid of what that decision will mean and how you can handle the change. Sometimes this is overthinking and ruminating. It takes a lot of energy. We have to remember that if we want to be happy, we have to make some moves.

What decision can you make today that will change your tomorrow for the better?

_____

_____

_____

_____

_____

_____

_____

* * *

Have you ever sat back and took the time to really examine your life and to look at the areas that cause you distress? It's funny, but when you do this as I have, you will realize 99.9% of the time, **YOU** are the reason for your distress. For example, if one of your areas of distress is a result of relationships, then 9.9 out of ten times **you** have allowed certain things to happen and **you** have allowed people to treat you a certain way.

If financial stability is an area of distress for you then again, 9.9 out of ten times, **you** hold the responsibility due to the inability to budget and the habit of overspending. It's not that you don't have enough, you just don't know how to manage what you have. In both examples, **you** have been the main theme and **you** will always be, which means the power to change lies within you.

I know the two following facts first-hand: 1) change isn't easy, and 2) you cannot force a person to change. But as you sit back and think about this, I want you to begin to **C**hallenge your own **H**abits and **A**ttitudes and begin to **N**ourish the new **G**rowth and **E**xpectations which will begin to take place in your life. I want to encourage you to make changes in the areas of your life you are not satisfied with. I know the concept seems simple but realistically speaking as far as execution is concerned, it's a process. Change doesn't happen overnight, but you have to start somewhere and only you know where that somewhere is. It's especially important for you not to worry about what others will think. Change takes place from within. Change because **YOU** want to and not because somebody else thinks you should!

Changes for me are often fueled by the need to be challenged and to accept critical feedback. It's also fueled by wanting to see and do something different in my life, wanting something better. The biggest opportunity is to embrace the challenge which change brings. I had to learn how to work through being uncomfortable with the actions needed to put me in a better place. The questions to ask are: 1) what do I need to put in my rearview mirror, 2) what experience/people that have shaped me, and 3) what is it I need to confront? If I continually have to confront change, then I have to look in the mirror and address self-esteem and the lack of confidence, self-love, and self-respect.

I made the decision to change my mindset. I had to get my mind to not focus on being a victim but being healed. From my experience, sitting with a victim mentality meant there was no growth. I was blaming the world and everyone I could find to have sympathy for me. I wanted to be the center of attention. I was craving compassionate attention instead of supportive attention.

Victimization will keep you in the state you are in. Once you make the decision to transform your negativity and blaming others mindset into a growth mentality, you will instantly begin to feel the effects of making positive changes and decisions that serve you and not someone else.

It took experience to change my beliefs on a lot of things. Looking back, if I saw my negative experiences as they were ... signs of growth, I would have confirmed long ago that they were needed to make me better. The changes that took place because of those experiences were good changes. I know now that negative experiences are tools for my growth. This is because, if I ever were to experience those situations again, I can make better decisions. Also, because of those negative experiences, I gained better decision-making skills that I can take with me in my everyday life. Changing my decision-making process helps me to continue growing in life.

Want to know the best part of decision-making? You always have the opportunity to change your mind ... and that is okay.

What decisions did you have to make to create a better environment for yourself?

_____

_____

_____

_____

_____

_____

_____

_____

_____

_____

_____

_____

_____

_____

_____

_____

_____

_____

SERVANT LEADERSHIP/PAY IT FORWARD

There is a difference between being a leader and being a servant leader. Many leaders that are in place are not truly leaders. Leading by example is one characteristic of a great leader, but a servant leader is ... to serve others, you must be humble and caring. Your legacy cannot move forward unless you pay it forward. The way to do this is by finding joy in elevating others.

There are mentors and there are sponsors. A mentor guides you and pushes you towards your goals. They share personal experiences and give you advice. They also give you the opportunity to explore things you may not have known about. They share their knowledge.

A sponsor takes mentoring to another level. A sponsor has all the characteristics of a mentor and extends it to deeper level of personal investment. They become active advocates for you by introducing you to critical thinking friends that can assist as well. Most sponsors are people of influence. They invest their time and money on a deeper level because they can see what you cannot see. This is for mentors and sponsors. You must present yourself worthy of their trust.

A servant leader serves others. They are people friendly that want to genuinely help others in need. It's not about 'me' it's about 'us'. Organizations often have organizational charts. These charts show the hierarchy of the company. At the top are the executives that have decision-making power and the people at the bottom of the chart are those that the organization may deem unimportant. What if we flipped that chart? What could happen then? Others become transformed and unity occurs. At that point, we are all equals. No one is better than the other. We can then work better, work smarter and not harder because we treat each other the same.

My mentors and sponsors are servant leaders. They saw me, and they wanted to help me. I allowed them to help. The greatest lesson I learned for all was to pay it forward. My sponsor is a Servant Leader requested that I do three things: To listen, to always be honest, and to pay it forward.

Have you ever been in a line at the grocery store or a restaurant and was the recipient of a good deed? Most times it happens when you're ready to pay for something. As you pull your money out, the cashier tells you that the person in front of you paid for you. Most often than not, that single act causes a chain reaction of good deeds. This is what paying it forward looks like.

Every day that I walk my dog, there are children outside that pet him and play with him. I even played a game or two with them like hopscotch and red-light-green-light. Those games are among the things I used to love as a child. On several occasions, I would play with the children and see another child at the end of the driveway playing by herself. I asked them why they are not playing with her. Their response was they tried to play with her, but she was a little weird.

The next day, I saw the same girl playing alone. When I passed her, she asked if she could pet my dog. Of course, I told her she could. I could see the joy on her face when she was petting Logan. She then explained that she wanted a dog but was unable to have one. When I asked her why, she said her mom said she couldn't. I asked her what her name was, and she told me, Sandy. That day, I continued my walk with Logan. As the day went and others came, I never forgot about Sandy.

The next time I saw her, I let her pet my dog again. This time I asked her why she didn't play with the other children. Her response, "Nobody likes me." At that moment, I knew Sandy was special. Sandy is different, it was not my job to try and diagnose her. My job was to love her. I learned that Sandy brings me joy. She has helped me discover the essence of who I truly am and the power I have inside of me.

Oftentimes, people ask me what brings me joy. I never had an answer for this question. Now I know that spending time helping others experience happiness. For example, Sandy brings me joy. Every time Sandy comes over to play with my dog, I see it being a special gift to her she will never forget. I became another person in her life that loves her and cares about seeing her happy.

After I graduated from College, I became a mentor to teen parents and other youth that had a goal to go to college. I invested what little I had in others. Someone invested in me, and it is my responsibility to pay it forward. Don't get me wrong, it's nice to buy a cup of coffee or a meal for a person behind you in a driveway line, but what about the person on the street that has been forgotten? What about others that don't have support?

~~~

L.C.'s story: LC was the first person I mentored. She was a teen mother that wanted to go to college. One day, I was a guest speaker and shared my story with a junior and senior class on College Readiness. At the end of the class, LC approached me, and shared her story. She wanted to go to college. She had a daughter, and her mother did not want her to leave home. I begin sharing resources with her. Like I was told, I told her that she could go to college, and take her daughter with her. She applied for the Gates Millennium Scholarship. This Scholarship paid her tuition all the way up to a doctorate. I was extremely proud of her. She eventually attended the same College I went to, Northern Illinois University. Excited for LC who now has this new perspective on life, I assisted her with moving from Chicago to Dekalb, Illinois. I made sure that she had furniture, food, and anything else she needed. It was my goal to help her with what seemed impossible. LC is now back in Chicago, has a master's degree, and is working on a doctorate. She is a teacher.

~~~

B's Story: B was in my classroom while I was a student teacher. I had the best mentor teacher and strived to be just like her. In the classroom, I was silly but engaged. Energetic to the students that did not have energy and a repository for essential care items that students may need. B was always in trouble. She was intelligent but lacked discipline. I did a home visit with B. She wanted me to meet her mother. What I learned, changed my perspective on her. Her mom had several other children. B was the oldest. After school, her routine wasn't homework. Her routine was to help her mother with her siblings. B did not know how to be a child. B did not know that she could have fun by herself. B did not know who she was until she met me. I spoke to her mom and asked her if B could stay with me during the summer. B spent the summer with me and my daughters experiencing life with girls around her age. I welcomed B into our home, and I treated her just like I treated my daughters. Though I don't know where B is today, I would like to think my small act of kindness had an impact on her life.

~~~

C.H.'s Story: CH was another one of my Chicago Public Schools mentees. I met him while I was doing a College Readiness Coaching visit. CH had an amazing gift of speaking. He was not afraid to talk about his life growing up on the Southside of Chicago. He also had a good understanding of his father's incarceration. CH and I naturally connected. I could see the greatness in him. I could see far beyond what he probably saw.

CH applied for and won the Gates Millenium Scholarship. That scholarship took him to Morehouse College. CH did well in college and well after. With a love for his community, CH developed a program that helped Morehouse Brother's serve in the community he lived in during spring break. This spring break tour, turned into one of the biggest African American Male programs in the City of Chicago. Yes, CH did that. CH learned the importance of giving back to the community. CH obtained his master's degree and is now working as a teacher in Chicago Public Schools. I am sticking like glue to CH, continuing to push him towards getting a doctorate. As I share with all my mentees that have that goal: A doctorate is tedious but doable. CH helped me develop my dissertation coaching for those who needed motivation and assistance.

~~~

K.T.'s Story: KT was a rockstar. I met her while she was in class listening to me speak. KT was also part of a Student Leadership program I facilitated. I loved all of my leadership students. I did not want them to think I was better than them, I wanted them to see that we were equals. I showed them how leadership skills could help them do better in school and life. I showed them the skills I needed to complete college as a single mother.

I remember that KT and I connected immediately. We kept in touch while she was in college, and I became her advocate. KT received a scholarship for college, but the funds were not released. The scholarship was critical to KT continuing in college. I knew the office that the scholarship came from, so I made a single phone call. Within weeks, KT's scholarship funds were credited to her school. KT could continue.

KT graduated from college but had a major problem returning to the city. She understood and was aware that moving back to Chicago was <u>not</u> an option. She wanted better and she wanted new. Things aligned perfectly. I was moving to Austin, and I invited KT to move with me. My oldest daughter left for college. Because I traveled for work, it was a nice exchange to have her help me with my youngest. KT and I had a great time together. We laughed together and had deep conversations. KT also did something for me. She helped my youngest daughter blossom from a place of low self-esteem and isolation, to being the confident, out-going personality she is today. She paid it forward to my daughter. I will never forget that. I will also never forget the kittens she bought home. We cared for them, just as we cared and supported each other. KT has graduated with a master's degree and married a handsome and an amazing young man.

~~~

L.F.'s Story: LF was introduced to me by one of my mentors. LF was a little younger than me, but I could see the light in his eyes. When I met LF, he was a great speaker and greatly confident. Though LF graduated from college, I knew he could do more. LF enrolled in school after considering what it was that he really wanted to do to serve African American males such as himself. LF had dreams of becoming a football player but met a significant obstacle trying to get there. That helped me understand that LF was resilient. He could do anything he put his mind to. LF finally decided to work on his master's degree. He was excited to share with me his first assignment. I coached him through how to complete it. With the next assignment LF brought me, I told him he needed to read in order to have a scholarly mindset. LF was resistant and thought I did not know what I was talking about. He stopped answering my calls and shared with me that he had someone else to help him. My standards for LF never changed. When he was ready to be challenged, I knew he would be back. LF came back to me with a new eye and a new level of maturity. LF learned that he needed to read, and he began reading. LF received his master's degree and is halfway done with his doctorate.

~~~

M.W.'s Story: MW is an amazing young man. He was interested in supporting students in college that did not have access to food. It was not until he shared his story that I understood why he was passionate about that. He was adamant about not returning to complete College. I met him where he was and coached him to do what brings him joy.

MW is also a strong networker. When he is in a room with people, he assesses those he wants to know about.

This has paid off for him many times over. I enjoyed watching him excel. He is now one of the top Real Estate Agents in the Dallas/Fort Worth Metroplex.

*   *   *

I have mentored and coached a lot of students over the years. I give them my personal cell phone number and encourage them to keep in touch, and to contact me if they needed support. Over the years, this support began spreading out to my daughter's friends and their friends. There are too many to count but it warms my heart that my decision to serve others paid off in major ways. I have been able to change the lives of those that may have felt they were less than.

I enjoy mentoring students and adults that have had similar experiences I did. It's important they have an example of someone who has made it through in spite of obstacles. Service is one of the biggest lessons of paying it forward. Each of my mentees know that I am not perfect, and we have conversations about that. At times, we struggle together. But the key word is 'together'.

Answer the following questions that would help you focus:

What brings you joy?

_____

_____

_____

_____

_____

_____

_____
_____
_____

What makes you happy?

_____
_____
_____
_____
_____
_____
_____
_____

What will you do to give back to the world?

_____
_____
_____
_____
_____
_____
_____
_____
_____
_____

THE ECLIPSE OF TIME

The greatest enemy of progress is your last success,
you could become so proud of what you've already
accomplished that you stop moving ahead to what you
can still accomplish.

~MYLES MUNROE

A solar eclipse occurs when the moon passes between the sun and the earth. The first solar eclipse I witnessed happened on August 21, 2017. When the eclipse happens, it looks like midnight for several minutes and then the sun peeks back out and it becomes day again.

On August 21, 2017, my youngest daughter began college. It was like déjà vu. Similar to my college story, my younger daughter was told by her high school teachers and counselors she would be unable to attend college. She did not meet the requirements for the college track curriculum. We were new to the area and new to the school district. Schools have been the reason I moved my children to specific neighborhoods. In spite of what we all went through, I wanted them to have the best education.

I was at the meeting where she was told that she would not be able to go to college in the state of Texas. Fortunately, they had no idea of who they were talking to. My patience for school staff members who discourage children from what they want to do is low. A child should not have to cry because an adult has blocked their future plans. When we tell students what they cannot do, instead of what they can is hurtful to their sense of self and their confidence. I could not sit in the meeting without saying something.

I went from being professional to being angry. My daughter put her head down because she knew what would happen next. I raised my voice, looked every person in the eye and told them they should never ever speak like that about students especially in front of a student.

In addition, I demanded they treat my daughter and any student as they would treat students that had the opportunity to tour colleges and take AP (advanced placement) and honors classes. We already knew that my daughter was not going to College in Texas.

My advocacy rant which I will never apologize went like this, "I am Dr. Valerie Peterson who is employed by your College Readiness Program. I don't want to ever hear you say, 'what a student cannot do'. Regardless of my ethnicity, degrees, and age, I deserve respect as a parent. Just like I advocate for other students, I will support mine."

What I wanted was them to respect my daughter and her wishes. Advocacy is the way I did it. Surprisingly, the next day, all the teachers and administrative staff knew who my daughter and I are.

I only had one other disagreement with the state. The TSIA (Texas Success Initiative Assessment) is part of the state law to determine whether or not a student is ready for college. Since I knew my daughter would not be attending school in Texas, I refused to let them keep testing her. The pressure of testing was devasting to my daughter and me as I watched her suffer. It caused her insomnia, panic, anxiety, feelings of not being good enough, and depression. I know the school cared about their track record of achievement and success. I cared for my daughter. No test score is greater than the child that took the test. I was not sorry if their scores did not change. It seemed dark like an eclipse for my daughter. The light came several months later when she was accepted at Kansas State University.

This was a practice that was not going to continue on the back of students that potentially could bring scores down. Our job as educators is to meet them where they are and to help them level up.

*   *   *

The eclipse was a turning point into the next phase of my life. While I initially thought the eclipse was a representation of my transition to new, it forced me to think about the areas of my life that needed fine tuning even if I did not want to acknowledge it.

When I want something, I want it now! I don't have the patience to wait. This is where I get into trouble.

When our goals and desires don't happen at the time, we want them to, we can begin to look down on ourselves and get sad. Delayed doesn't mean denied. What we need will come to us when we aren't looking.

We cannot respond because there was or is an incident. Our response should be to establish a precedent, whether it's for ourselves or others. In other words, we must be proactive instead of reactive. When you have a sense or awareness of timing, you will know when the time is right. The timing has to be right for you because you're the one who matters.

With the right timing you can embrace and implement anything. If no one gives you an opportunity, create one.

When you have surrendered, you will know the timing is right. Your intentions become pure. Your focus and clarity sharpen. You will move without hesitation. Sure, you may have some competing thoughts, or unanswered questions but when the timing is right, everything falls into place.

When thinking about timing, even when things go wrong, it's important to stay ready and have your plan of action prepared.

In 2017, I had a partial hysterectomy. I had cysts on my ovaries that were large and painful. I also learned that my kidney and liver had small cysts as well. My hair was falling out. I had locs that were thinning. I found out I may have an autoimmune disease. I have alopecia areata a rare condition that attacks the hair follicles. My hair was not coming back.

In 2018, my body and my mental health broke down. I was troubled by a negative work experience that created a toxic environment. I took a leave of absence to address my mental health.

I had back pain for years that was not addressed. It hurt to stand. I found out I had spinal stenosis and had surgery on L3, L4, L5 and S1 of my spine. My weight was out of control. My spine surgeon told me to avoid a spinal fusion, I needed to get the weight off my back. Due to the limited time I had to lose it, I opted for the gastric sleeve. Now with 120 pounds off my back, I could breathe again. sleep apnea ... gone, high blood pressure ... gone. Health, wellness, exercise, and enjoying nature by walking renewed my life and the sense of who I am.

By 2019, I was working at another job thinking I was new and refreshed. I was still going through tough times. In 2020, I lost that job, and I lost my Dad. As a result, I ended up in the rabbit hole. I needed help because I did not know how to cope! Though I could not see the end at that time when I finally became aware of it, I realized that it was something that I needed to go through in order to position myself for success. I am thankful for my rabbit hole experiences.

In 2020, we had the pandemic and a lot of our loved ones died. We were cut off from our friends, family, and other loved ones. We were stuck in the house and forced to deal with the decisions that were made over time.

In May 2021, we had a lunar eclipse which signaled time for a new beginning. I choose to use the pandemic as a growth tool. I made risks that I never would have made if my mindset didn't change. I was forced to accept aspects of my personality that were keeping me stuck. I was being held accountable. The only person I would let down was myself.

This time I was aligned with my purpose, and I was ready to do some leveling up of myself. I gained a renewed sense of self. I bet on myself and everything I have invested over the years is coming to fruition. Life is a journey. A beautiful weave of the positive and the negative. Now I can take negatives, get support, and learn the lesson. I share the lessons I have learned with everyone I meet. Life is a give and take. Enjoy the ride while you can.

A REFLECTION FROM ONE OF MY MENTORS

When asked to do this "chapter" I was honored and excited and a million ideas flooded my brain. The entire essay was laid out and done. This was going to be easy. Although, I wish I had recorded all those incidents as they materialized. I would not have had the brain freeze experience. I had more questions than ideas! Where should I start? What should I say? How shall I say it? What shouldn't I say? Do I remember incidents clearly? So, I decided to start with a little background information to set the stage and fill the page.

~PAMELA NORFLEET (AUNT PAM)

My relationship with Valerie is rooted in the church. In those days the church, Valerie's family, my family, and dozens of other families who attended were family oriented. We were all remarkably close and there were lots of children and babies. The years from 1978 to 1980 were particularly fruitful in our lives. Most of the babies born during that period still remain friends or at least keep in touch with each other to this day. Looking back, we were almost communal with the caring of our babies during church.

The nursery was covered by two or three moms or related volunteers. We would rotate each week with chosen partners on nursery duty so the moms could have an enjoyable time in the church service. In order to earn that hour or two of peace, you had to volunteer to be on the rotation roster. Fortunately, there were so many families involved, we served nursery duty maybe only twice a year. Thus, every child had several "Aunties".

There were also lots of outside activities that brought the families together, further fortifying lasting relationships. Valerie's mom, Veronica was one of my closest friends. During the baby blitz, Veronica and Solomon Peterson adopted their third child.

I remember the day Valerie was presented for her Baby Dedication. Most mothers dressed their babies in a fancy white outfit for their special day. Veronica just did the max! She made a full elaborate christening dress, oops ... gown for Baby Valerie. The gown was at least three times as long as the baby. It was beautiful and Valerie was exquisite! She looked like a baby doll.

She had velvety chocolate skin and dark eyes that sparkled in a round face framed by an antique lace cap. The outfit was the talk of the church for a long time and never duplicated. This was only a hint of just how unique and blessed Valerie was. She was the baby of her family and, according to her siblings, the spoiled favorite.

Growing up, Valerie was involved in the Children's Choir, Sunday School programs, and all holiday programs. In my memory she was always inquisitive, articulate, and intelligent. She smiled a lot even when her front teeth were prematurely lost and replaced with silver spacers until her permanent teeth grew in. I suppose she shrugged off the teasing (if any) and just kept smiling.

I was blessed to be the proud mother of five handsome and intelligent boys, (no shame here), and Valerie was one of my many "play daughters".

Chronologically, Valerie's age fell between my third and fourth son. I was quite involved with activities and schoolwork with my boys and most of my friends were busy with their own children. Occasionally, we would brag over their academic achievements, prowess in sports, or accomplishments in the arts. Not that we were in competition, we were just proud of our children.

My boys were all honor roll students and Veronica always made sure I was kept informed of all Valerie's many accomplishments. I think perhaps during her elementary school years I began to be impressed with her grades, and her writing abilities. Valerie was also an avid reader. I discovered Valerie liked to journal ... we were kindred spirits! I myself loved to read and fancied myself a writer and poet, and I too loved to journal! The bond was beginning between us.

My memory fails to reconstruct the exact event which led to my first talk with Valerie. I think it might have been sparked by a journal entry her Mom had read and got upset.

There was a closely knit group of confidants who would often discuss our frustrations, disappointments, or what made us angry with our children, (and husbands). Veronica would have come to us, or me alone to vent. Whatever the start, it grew to be a very personal and deep relationship. I know that as parents, Solomon and Veronica doted on their children and expected only the best from them, (a common parental condition), especially Valerie. I also know that sometimes parents are often in denial or turn a blind eye and a deaf ear to any hint of an unpleasant flaw in their children.

I do know our relationship intensified when Val became pregnant with her older daughter. It was just another similarity in our lives. I too had become pregnant in my senior year of High School. I had known she was sexually active and encouraged her to talk with her mother. I even threatened to tell her myself. I held off because in my heart I knew what Valerie was going through.

My story was so similar when I was her age, and I had not a soul to turn to. I felt she needed to have someone she could talk to and trust. Ironically, with all the church background a lot of people have, they are often alone with "earthly" dilemmas and problems because "the church" is so often the most unforgiving.

Some "Church Folk" forget that they weren't born "saved". They forget the things they did as children or even adults that would not be pleasing in God's sight. They sit high and look low, criticizing and judging and ultimately chasing people, especially young people, away from not only the church ... but from God.

Valerie was afraid, and embarrassed. At this point, I was merely a confidant, not a mentor, teacher, counselor or even a rational adult. I was emotionally invested in a happy outcome for her and her baby. I was just reliving my own experience but determined to not let her be alone in hers. I did a lot of praying for her. I was even present in the delivery room to witness the birth of her oldest daughter. She chose my husband and I to be Godparents.

We all took a deep breath and a refreshing exhale when Valerie graduated with honors and went to college. Provisions were even made for her to attend college with her daughter. All was well with our world ... not Valerie's.

I think what we all missed was the fact that Valerie was overwhelmed with trying to please everyone by keeping the façade of the smart, happy, little church girl alive and well. She was now a mother and a college student. Yes, there were acceptance and support, but at her core there were fear, loneliness, and depression. I will not go into depth with the perils, pitfalls, and another pregnancy Valerie experienced while in college. That is her story to tell. I, by this time, had grown into the role of confidant, encourager, admonisher, but mostly a listener.

I worried about her, prayed for her, and on occasion wondered if she had lost her @!#*!! mind!

Through each phase and episode of her risings and plunges, I tried to encourage, listen, and remind her that she was worthy of love and blessings. On the outside she was indeed a warrior. It seemed she was conquering every obstacle in her path. Often, she was her own obstacle. Certain addictions intensified her depression. One particularly horrifying incident she told me about almost made me lose it. I couldn't believe she thought this would be gratifying without consequences! This was the first time that I felt all hope was gone. I was disappointed and afraid for not only her, but the safety her children as well. I think that was a "rock bottom" moment for her and it wasn't the last one. I am going to try and wrap this up because this is not my story (feels like it).

Valerie has been through so much and yet her background and trials are not unique. Her spirit, courage, and strong will are commendable. She is blessed and highly favored. Each trial, tragedy, and disappointment she has experienced has been a brick in the building of a strong, new, beautiful, intelligent, and confident woman. I believe her story is one of hope, ambition, and inspiration to the women and girls of color who recognize themselves in Valerie's narrative. The happy ending for today's Black women is not limited to the proverbial happy marriage and a happily ever after. They can have that, if they want it, and have confidence, power, freedom, fearlessness, and the knowledge that they too are blessed and highly favored!

I am so proud of what Valerie has accomplished and eager to see what new heights she will soar!

GRACE FROM MY MOTHER'S HEART

By Veronica Peterson

There have always been letters from Valerie on my pillow. The earliest letter I can remember was about how much she loved me and her dad and apologized for not cleaning her room. She thanked me for adopting her.

I too was thankful that I was able to adopt a newborn. This helped me raise her from the beginning. I was able to teach her, her alphabets, reading, writing, colors, shapes, numbers, and also how to take care of herself. I did that with all my children.

When there was a dance in high school or a football game she wanted to attend, she would always write a letter that she cleaned her room.

This one was the last letter and a biggie too. Again, she wrote how much she loved me and her dad. She was sorry she disappointed us when she got pregnant at 17. Valerie always told us being pregnant would not stop her from graduating from high school and college. She was also confident in knowing she would be a medical doctor. All of the above came true, completed high school, received Bachelor of Science, Master's of Education. She may not be a medical doctor, but she received her Doctorate in Education.

One of our experiences was when Valerie and I were in Target, and we ran into Pam. I did not believe that Valerie was in labor. Since I had never been in labor, I did not know. Pam had to tell me to take Valerie to the hospital. Valerie had her first born in the hospital examining room. The doctor and nurses had just got her in the delivery room and Kenedi was born.

Val always accomplished whatever she set out to do. Working as a teacher, working in various non-profits, and now she has a company of her own ... and of course, the book. She has been working on forever.

People said she could not do it raising two children on her own, but yes, she did. Val has taken us on fantastic vacations. Now we are starting a new chapter in our lives here in Vegas after the death of my husband, her dad. Her and I relocated here – a place where we both dreamed of living. Nothing can stop her.

A fond memory of Val, whenever she wanted to go somewhere, she would clean the house so well I thought I had cleaned it. Since she went away to college, we would sometimes help with her daughters to give her a break. My husband and I also kept them for three years to help her out while she was working on her master's and doctorate.

Val is a very caring and a loving daughter. No one could ask for a better daughter. She has single-handedly put both of her daughters through college. There is no greater love than the love you get from your children.

I am fortunate to have raised a child that knew and was determined to be successful.

I LOVE YOU, DADDY

~~~

A TRIBUTE TO MY FATHER

Daddy, my new angel from above (though you were my angel on earth) you were selfless, you were strong, but most of all, you were a provider. You knew your purpose! You never judged, you only loved and supported. You have always been God's favorite and his favor transferred through you, radiated with showers of love, and light which transformed the lives of many outside of our home. I take great comfort in knowing you are wrapped around the arms of God right where you were ready to be. Soon and very soon ... it's never goodbye, only see ya later. I love you always.

~VALERIE

Growing up I remember early Saturday mornings where I would awake to the fresh aroma of breakfast.

The smell of buttered toast coming from the oven graced my nose. The smoky smell of bacon, sausage, or smoked sausage did as well ... take your pick. I heard the bubbling of the buttery grits and the smell of eggs. The countdown would begin as I listened to the plates clank around the kitchen. 'Breakfast is ready' is what my Mother or Father yelled out. These were the sweet morning sounds of my house. We always prayed over our food. My Mom or Dad's prayer would go like this, "Thank you Lord for the food we're about to receive. Let it be nourishment and a blessing for the body. In Jesus's name, Amen."

My Dad would then head off to work driving the bus for the Chicago Transit Authority (CTA), as I mentioned earlier, and my mom frantically running about to make sure my brother, sister, and I would make it to school on time.

I was sickly as a baby ... struggling to breathe stricken with a severe form of asthma. For me that meant long hospital stays and multiple trips to the doctor. My inhaler was my best friend and the smell of Vicks Vapor Rub lived in my nostrils. My body would often be weak. Whenever I was sick, my dad would rub Vicks® VapoRub™ on my back and put it in a humidifier.

As a child in addition to dealing with asthma, I had a lisp. I also had vision problems and underwent eye therapy. I also had to wear these big goofy looking glasses people would tease me about. To this day, one of my friends calls and asks me when I was last in the hospital. It was pretty funny but also real. My Mother and

Father would always take care of me especially my Dad when I got home from school.

The care from my dad was there as I continued to grow up. He never saw how I could make it through college as a single mom, but he believed in me and somehow had the foresight to know I would always be okay. With that said, my dad brought me a car. However, I will never forget the white couch he gave me that he found in one of the expensive neighborhoods in the city. He was proud of it and so was I ... until he told me he got it from an Alley in the neighborhood.

Adjusting to College was hard and my dad recognized it. So much so, he would often come to my apartment to clean the house and do the laundry. I could always count on my white clothes to be pink. My Dad would also perm my hair and sometimes shaved it too high in the back. My Dad loved to do hair.

My father was a hardworking man. He taught me how to drive using the grid system in Chicago. He would have me get lost on purpose.

My dad was a God-fearing man. His foundation was based on the apostolic doctrine and biblical foundations.

My dad was a supporter. Though he watched from afar, he was there to celebrate my successes.

As I mentioned previously, on April 10, 2020, was one of the worst of several bad days of my life. On this day, my Father succumbed to complications from the novel (new) COVID-19 virus. I was living in Dallas at the time and did not have the opportunity to see my Father during his illness and after his death because of the travel restrictions, health precautions, and possible quarantining implications of traveling from state to state during the beginning of the pandemic. It would not be until August of 2020; I would be able to travel to Chicago with my daughters to attend my dad's grave and to see my family for the first time since my Dad's death. This was one of the most difficult moments of my life. I was grieving for my first love ... my Daddy.

A Letter to my Father

Dear Daddy,

I told you I was going to get it right this time. I'm finally walking along the right path. It's amazing how everything I know to be good and comfortable has to break into pieces before I can get up and recognize the fact, I have work to do. I speak from experience. Experiences have happened from the time I was born until now. I've taken the rollercoaster ride many times. Up, down, fast, slow, full stop. Each and every time you were there. You were there to guide me and to pick me up.

It hurts me to know I couldn't be there with you when you took your last breath. I couldn't be there to comfort you as you battled the complications of COVID-19 and lay in a hospital room all alone with doctors and nurses wearing what probably looked like a spacesuit to you.

Though I was comforted and at peace pretty early during the grieving process, I knew your time was coming just as you had voiced over the years. I also knew you were ready. You had a picture of angels with the phrase "soon and very soon" on the lock screen of your cellphone. This was no mistake and I know God doesn't make mistakes.

If angels have wings, they have feathers. When I opened the car door at the cemetery the very first thing, I saw on the ground was a long feather. I looked at the feather, picked it up and smiled. I kept the feather and the many others I have seen since then. There are tons of feathers around me, and I know this is you reminding me you are right by my side.

I was comforted in knowing you departed physically from this world, and I had no regrets. Our relationship was solid. The last thing you heard me say was I love you. Now I know you're guiding me … you're guiding me from the other side and man-o-man, what a ride this is. You always told me I was blessed. You always told me I have favor and most importantly you told me and taught me God is in love with me. I get it now. I see it and I'm going to get it right this time. You've already seen what I can't yet see. I'm excited for the newness, and I know you are right by my side. I love you forever! The imprint you have left on my heart and on my life is big. I'm glad you chose me to be your daughter. I will never forget that just like I will never forget you.

I honor you and I love you! I will be everything you saw in me to be.

Sincerely,

Your girl, Dr. Val 🙂

Journal Entry ~ August 18, 2020:

<u>A Note to My Father</u>

Today is the first day I have stepped in the house since your death. I felt your presence as soon as I walked through the door. Your energy was strong and soothing, but I couldn't help but to break down and cry. Kenedi was there to give me a big hug and it meant a lot and was needed. I have mixed emotions right now. I miss the smell of boiling water with a ham hock in it as I walk through the door where I remember your hands extended to welcome me. I miss seeing you physically, but I know you are here spiritually as I can hear your voice from within. You told me while I was sitting in your favorite chair, "You are strong, and you have everything you need to continue moving forward. This is nothing but a bump in the road, but I can do more for you walking with God that I couldn't do for you physically on earth. It's time for you to reset and refocus, realize the strength you have. As you continue to transition and grow for the next chapter of your life, don't panic, you got this."

I left and returned on another day and recall that mom had finished preparing your last batch of collard greens then we ate them together. This reminded me of how great of a chef you were.

207

SELF-AWARENESS

Letter to myself: *Dear Val, you are an amazing, beautiful, and smart woman. You have achieved things no one thought was possible. You were determined and you survived. Now, one of the biggest tasks in front of you is to acknowledge and become more aware of your worth. You are extremely precious and should only spend your time, thoughts, and energies on the things and people who respect you. The time for settling is over. You are good enough and now you deserve to be treated as such and to recognize your worth!*

When I think about self-awareness now, I think about it in terms of an onion which has many layers. I need to think about why I feel like I am suffering and what emotions are attached to that. There are times what we do and say comes from *ignorant innocence*. Ignorance is the lack of knowledge about something.

Ignorant innocence is where we have a belief that we know about something but yet, we don't have enough experience. Not being able to talk from experience and believing what we say and do without having proof of the action creates ignorant innocence.

We may be ignorant in thinking there is only one way to get through to the other side. There is always more than one way to get there. We are not always aware of some of the microaggressions we make toward others, and there are times we are not aware and can never control how others see us. Developing self-awareness is like creating solid muscles or a six pack. We have to exercise the muscle by thinking for ourselves and asking for clarity when there are things that don't make sense to us. This is when critical thinking becomes more critical.

When I look at myself and ask the question, "Why are you suffering?" I can begin to pull back the layers of the onion. Layer one is about emotions, layer two is questioning why I am feeling those emotions, and layer three is what are my personal values?

Ask yourself the following:

1. Why am I suffering?
2. What emotions am I feeling and why?
3. What are my personal values I need to uphold?

Random Journal entry ~ 2017

Confidence is internal. You can't buy your way to love. You have to love yourself first and then take time to learn somebody else. We want to be loved, we want to give or feel like we are helping someone else.... But what about helping ourselves. I have spent too much time being the supporter and the caregiver in relationships. Now it's time to consider me. It is my time to be taken care of and to receive. I deserve it and there is nothing wrong with it being that way.

Now, what action will you take?

_____
_____
_____
_____
_____
_____
_____
_____
_____

Know this is a journey. Nothing will ever be perfect; no one will ever be perfect. I am still working through some of the issues I shared with you. Together, we can make things more tolerable by changing the script and incorporating prayer and meditation to our daily routine. It's time to get off the ground, get out the rabbit hole that is still easy to fall into.

Now join me in this prayer:

"Dear God, please take all of the situations in my life that make me weep, anxious, and fear the worst-case scenario.

I want to learn how to stay in the present and acknowledge the gifts I have right now.

Help me learn how to navigate this journey because only the experiences you give me, can make me stronger.

I must get rid of my ego and those things that are not profitable to create more space for your presence and your love.

Teach me God, to learn how to ask for help, so I can be in a position to love. Create space in my life for those that need me and will be drawn to me."

And it is so!

Living a legacy is developing people so they can have a dream for themselves. Sam Cooke is in the grave, but we still sample and listen to his music. Michael Jordan's shoes will always be worth something ... most likely worth even more when he passes away. Maya Angelou is resting in the arms of God, yet we still use her poems and messages just as I did earlier in the book.

FOR MY DAUGHTERS

(Certainly not Least)

Kenedi and Devin, my heart is full of joy! I admire your resilience as we navigated more than 20 years of tougher times than good times. I have enjoyed the journey of seeing y'all grow and mature. I laugh at the things that you do, that I did. You have become just like me because you finally understand the 'why'.

I always explained that both of you capture me. Kenedi, you have my serious, nurturing side, and Devin, the chill, dare devil, fun, playful side of me.

Kenedi my favorite memory of you is when you sung through the instrumental of 'The Boy is Mine'. At two years old, you knew the tune and chorus perfectly. I also enjoyed watching you throughout the love you had for Blue's Clues. Thank you for filling in when I could not care for Devin, a responsibility that should have never been yours.

Devin, I remember how you used to crawl under the pews at church. As a baby, I used to sneak under tables and play with people's feet so, I guess you got it from me. Though you hate it when I talk about it, the bike lock story was epic. Thank you for teaching me patience and understanding. I should have been teaching this to you. Proof that we can learn valuable lessons from children.

From young babies to beautiful young ladies with my cheekbones, heart, and smile, it warms my heart to see the accomplishments that you both made. Kenedi, you have been dancing, singing, and cheering since you were in my womb. Becoming a dance therapist is what you were born to be. Devin, you admired the clouds and taking photos since you were young. You are now a professional photographer and your dream of owning your own business has begun.

It has not been smooth sailing from communication issues, to trust issues, to us all trying to figure out our personal identities but, you both adjusted every time. You have seen and experienced a lot of things that you should not have as young children, yet you emerged and grew alongside me. You are both lotuses You can recognize the roots and use experience as fertilizer to continue to grow in healthy ways. You know and possess the tools to move forward. I cannot stress enough how proud I am of you. This is our time. This is what we have manifested for years. I think you both get it now ☺.

I love you both and look forward to our tomorrow as we continue to walk together.
~LOVE MOM

Dear Abundantly blessed (Val),

Great job on the effortless move and special congratulations on the completion of your book! As you've declared, this book has already taken you further than you've ever imagined. You are indeed blessed and have favor with God.

I also want to commend you on getting your finances under control. Having the ability to pay for Kenedi's college expenses is something you no longer must worry about.

You have transitioned well into your new home and life. Your daughters have adjusted well also. This has been an effortless change and I know the favor of God resting upon your life is what made it easy. Never forget where you came from and never forget those who have helped you. Continue your emotional healing work and know I'm with you always. It is so!

Yours truly,

*~**VALERIE***

NOW YOU KNOW ME

Never share a story of your life for pity. That does nothing but draw more pity and it gets you nowhere. The purpose of pain is experience. Experience to know how something feels and the experience of figuring out what to do next. You tell your story to heal. To vocalize your truth. This experience will answer the whys in your life; however, be aware it may take some time, years in some cases, to understand why you needed pain to take the next step in your life.

No matter where you are in the world, you are loved. No matter how the world sees you, you are loved. You have more than enough. You already know this. Remember to live in the present moment. Remember to live reality instead of fantasy. It's what it is. Life is too short to be stressed out by things you cannot control. Always keep God first and foremost in all you do. When you do, you never have to suffer. This is a mindset change. Remember, all the pain you have endured has given you a purpose and a reason to never give up. All is well and remember the law of least effort, everything you need will come to you effortlessly.

Now my question to you is, "How can I help you?"

_____
_____
_____
_____
_____
_____
_____
_____
_____
_____
_____
_____
_____
_____
_____
_____
_____
_____
_____
_____
_____
_____

BIOGRAPHY
DR. VALERIE R. PETERSON

Dr. Valerie R. Peterson was born and raised on the Southside of Chicago. Obtained a Bachelor of Science at Northern Illinois University (NIU) in DeKalb, Illinois.

Valerie went on to receive a master's degree in Elementary Education from Roosevelt University and a Doctoral Degree in Organizational Leadership from Argosy University, in Chicago.

Through mentoring and sharing her personal stories of success, failure, and the importance of individual determination, Valerie is a nationally recognized Professional Speaker, Consultant and Advocate for Social Justice, Public Education and Criminal Justice Reform. She works with people across the nation helping them break through barriers and achieve the goals they set for themselves through her Blue Lotus Consulting firm.

LOGAN